PRAISE F
FAITH AMONG THE ~~FAITHLESS~~

"'Be a Daniel' is the go-to-phrase for encouraging Christians to impact our culture. Mike Cosper turns this mantra on its head by looking to Esther to figure out our world. A brother looking to Esther, I love it! He gets it because Esther has the guts and the grit that we all need to bend the times to Christ."

—Kyle Idleman, pastor and author of *Not a Fan* and *Grace Is Greater*

"Mike Cosper gives us a finely written, timely, and sometimes provocative commentary on the themes of Esther. He retells the story with particular emphasis on how her story is really our own in a highly secularized society. I want an authentic witness in today's world and this commentary will help you to live and tell Christian truth in a non-Christian world."

—Ed Stetzer, Billy Graham Distinguished Chair, Wheaton College

"*Faith Among the Faithless* reveals rich and timely parallels between the ancient biblical story of Esther and the current time Christians find ourselves in. Deftly weaving these threads together, Mike Cosper creates a rich and illuminating tapestry of timeless biblical truth. It's been a long time since I have been so informed, inspired, and encouraged by a contemporary examination and application of a biblical narrative."

—Karen Swallow Prior, author of *Booked* and *Fierce Convictions*

"Mike Cosper is one of only a few Christian authors today who can match meaningful, insightful commentary with a sense of craft and artistry. This is why I'm honored to recommend *Faith Among the Faithless* to you, not simply as a guide to wisely navigating our tumultuous times but as an excellent reminder that the beauty of God's gospel has always overpowered the lures of this fallen world."

—Jared Wilson, director of content strategy at Midwestern Baptist Theological Seminary, managing editor of For The Church, and author of *Supernatural Power for Everyday People*

"We may live in a world gone mad, but that's not a new development. So long as you and I or our ancestors have walked this earth, sin has followed close behind. We need wisdom and grace to walk by faith among the faithless. You'll love how Mike Cosper retells the timeless story of Esther with details and perspectives you hadn't before considered. We need this book's vision of courageous faith in the face of assimilation."

—Collin Hansen, editorial director for The Gospel
Coalition and coauthor of *A God-Sized Vision*

"Few things resonate more powerfully than someone reminding you of who you are. *Faith Among the Faithless* plants the truth of scripture into our modern moment. With power, clarity, and conviction Mike Cosper clarifies the Christian response in our cultural moment."

—Gabe Lyons, president of Q and author of *Good Faith*

"Mike Cosper's latest work is a brilliant and timely walk through the book of Esther. From the moment I started reading this book, I could not put it down. In *Faith Among the Faithless* Cosper ushers the reader into the biblical account and shows how the message of Esther is a beam of light for a follower of Jesus navigating the current culture. I hope every Christian reads this book!"

—Brian Howard, chairman of the board of Acts 29
and founder of Context Coaching

FAITH
Among
THE
FAITH
LESS

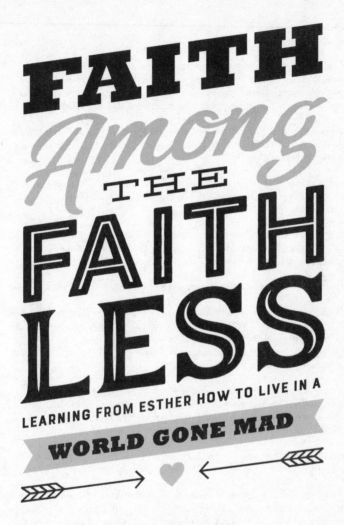

FAITH Among THE FAITH LESS

LEARNING FROM ESTHER HOW TO LIVE IN A WORLD GONE MAD

MIKE COSPER

NELSON
BOOKS

An Imprint of Thomas Nelson

Published in Nashville, Tennessee, by Nelson Books, an imprint of Thomas Nelson. Nelson Books and Thomas Nelson are registered trademarks of HarperCollins Christian Publishing, Inc.

Thomas Nelson titles may be purchased in bulk for educational, business, fund-raising, or sales promotional use. For information, please e-mail SpecialMarkets@ ThomasNelson.com.

ISBN 978-0-7180-9748-6 (eBook)

Library of Congress Cataloging-in-Publication Data

ISBN 978-0-7180-9747-9
Library of Congress Control Number: 2017954539

Printed in the United States of America

18 19 20 21 22   LSC   10 9 8 7 6 5 4 3 2 1

FOR HAROLD BEST

CONTENTS

FINDING OURSELVES IN A WORLD GONE MAD

On a hot June day, with green skies and swirling winds, I found myself stuck at the Denver airport, my flight home crawling through a series of delays that would ultimately lead to cancellation. I made my way to a restaurant with an indoor patio overlooking one of the airport's central hubs and began writing down some thoughts that had been stirring for a while—thoughts about the book of Esther, and how it might illuminate a way of life for Christians in a culture people have called a "secular age" and "post-Christian."

A year later, on another hot summer day, I was stuck once again in the Denver airport, awaiting a long-delayed flight. I took the time to look over my thoughts on Esther and culture. This time, though, the manuscript was pretty much finished.

It seemed oddly poetic to begin and end this book in an airport. Airports are in-between places, liminal spaces, thresholds that lead us to and from honeymoons, vacations, funerals, sales meetings, and the glories and miseries of work. They are also (as I know all too well) places of unpredictability, much like our world.

Consider the cultural shifts of the last decade. We've seen the expansion of gay rights and the rise of the alt-right. We've elected the first African-American president and we've elected Donald Trump. Christian schools, bakers, and florists have faced litigation for their beliefs and practices. Meanwhile, a conservative justice who nearly all assume is committed to the cause of religious liberty was easily confirmed to the Supreme Court. Even as I sat finalizing this manuscript, there were images of neo-Nazis and white supremacists marching around the city of Charlottesville, Virginia. By the day's end, one of them would slam a car into a crowd of protestors, injuring several and killing one.

I didn't see any of this coming, and it leads me to ask: Where are we headed? What comes next?

The world seems to be alternatingly progressive and regressive, and neither movement seems to be getting any closer to creating a world of peace and flourishing. Nor does either movement harmonize well with the way of life and understanding of the world described in the Bible. It seems most certainly a post-Christian world, but it isn't yet clear exactly what kind of world that is.

Within the Christian community, debates are taking place about the posture that Christians should take in this in-between space. Some think we should grasp once again for power and "take back" the cultural influence and cachet that's been lost in the last few decades. Others, seeing things in a bleaker light, are calling for a well-considered withdrawal, focusing on shoring up our institutions and preparing for the new dark ages that modern decadence is sure to bring upon us.

I confess I'm sympathetic to the latter view. I do think things are going to get worse before they get better. In spite of signs to the contrary, secularism marches on, and it will continue to apply pressure on churches and ordinary Christians, both in resisting their beliefs and undermining their place in the public sphere. There's some wisdom in saying, "Dear Christian: brace yourself."

But it's also true that this has always been the posture of Christians in the broader world. Christians have always served a different King and a different kingdom, and every generation faces the temptation to compromise—whether it concerns sexual ethics, racism and human dignity, or the ever-present lure of power and money.

And of course, compromise is never confined to one single issue. Today, we're immersed in a secular age, and we're profoundly shaped by its values—its consumerism, its addictive nature, its pleasure and distraction seeking. A way forward in such a world will be countercultural in a host of ways.

SEARCHING FOR A ROLE MODEL

Many who have examined our current cultural situation have looked to the prophet Daniel as a role model. Daniel found himself living in pagan Babylon and pressured on all sides to compromise, but he endured that pressure and lived to tell the tale, unstained by the culture around him. He bore witness to God's faithfulness, and he won a certain respectability and plausibility for Jews in the process.

But there's a problem with looking to Daniel: Most of us aren't a Daniel. In fact, we are far from it. As much as we recognize that our culture is in decline, we also kind of . . . like it. Christians in general consume as much mass media and are as addicted to pornography, as likely to divorce, as consumeristic, and as obsessed with social media as the rest of our world. Again: we're immersed in a secular age, and it's had a profound effect upon us.

Daniel's faith was iron-clad. He never let the pressure of exile shake his faith, and he didn't adopt the dominant culture's way of life. I wish that were me, but it's not. I'm not a Daniel. I—like many of us, I suspect—am more troubled than Daniel. Less steely. Like the old hymn says, I am "prone to wander,"[1] prone to moments of grey doubt that leave me wondering how certain I am about the things I think I believe and value most.

Daniel, on the other hand, was rooted in a countercultural way of life. Most scholars think he was taken into exile when he was about fifteen, which means he had spent most of his formative years in a Jewish world, immersed in the rhythms of the Jewish religion. He had a frame of reference for resistance in Babylon, clinging to his heritage and upbringing in the midst of a hostile world. And while he's a great model of faithfulness, I'm not sure he's the best reference point for most of us.

With that in mind, let me suggest an alternative to the Daniel model: someone born into exile, disconnected from a heritage of faith, out of touch with the practices that marked her people as distinct from the surrounding world. One who nonetheless found a way back to her identity as one of God's people, and one who might illustrate a path forward for the rest of us.

I am talking about Esther, but not the Esther you may think you know. I'm talking about the real Esther—the biblical and historical Esther—whose life was a whirlwind of spiritual compromise and spiritual awakening, and whose story is full of power, sex, and violence.

This is the Esther whose great moment is marked not by a show of force, but by vulnerability. The climax of her story comes when, after weakening her body with three days and nights of fasting, she walks a path that could most likely end in her death, in hopes of saving God's people.

Esther's story reveals a way forward in a culture where people of faith find themselves at the margins of society. She neither clutches for power nor seeks self-protection. Instead, she faces reality, embraces weakness, and finds faith, hope, and help from a world unseen.

Her story is also an invitation to those whose faith, convictions, and morality are less than they wish they were.

LESS *VEGGIETALES*, MORE *GAME OF THRONES*

Most of us know Esther's story from Sunday school lessons, storybooks, and cartoons. But there's a real problem with most of these versions. They're mostly wrong. Not all of them. Just most of them.

They make Esther sound like Daniel. They present her as if she is a pillar of virtue, a gorgeous, dignified Jewish girl who wins the heart of the king through the beauty, humility, and character imparted to her by her noble cousin Mordecai. When a crisis comes, she is more than ready to sacrifice herself for the Jewish people, confident that doing God's will is more important than saving her own skin.

At the very least, her story is more complicated than that. And much darker. It's less *VeggieTales* and more *Game of Thrones*, with a lot more sex, murder, and impaling than the usual version of the story would imply. (There's actually quite a bit of impaling.) Mordecai and Esther's motivations are sometimes murky and sometimes blatantly self-serving. Unquestionably, Esther and her cousin are profoundly compromised people when we meet them, having abandoned most of their Jewish identity for a Persian one.

Martin Luther hated the book of Esther, wanting it struck from the canon. He said, "I am so great an enemy to the second book of the Maccabees, and to Esther, that I wish they had not come to us at all, for they have too many heathen unnaturalities. The Jews much more esteemed the book of Esther than any of the prophets; though they were forbidden to read it before they had attained the age of thirty, by reason of the mystic matters it contains."[2]

For Luther, it was too Jewish, too heathen, and too scandalous. Yet these characteristics are what make the book so interesting.

Aside from Luther's anti-Semitism (though one should be extremely wary of glibly setting that aside), the "too Jewish" charge is an interesting one. An annual feast called Purim commemorates the story of Esther, and in some communities, it's the most celebrated feast and biggest party of the year. Why is that?

One answer is because for much of the history of the Jewish people, from Esther's day to our own, Jews lived without a land of their own. They were in exile, looking for hope, for the promise that Yahweh hadn't abandoned them. That's the whole point of the story of Esther. Even in the darkest moments, when God seems absent, we can trust that he hasn't abandoned us.

Novelist Walker Percy once wrote, "Why does no one find it remarkable that in most world cities today there are Jews but not one single Hittite, even though the Hittites had a great flourishing civilization while the Jews nearby were a weak and obscure people?"[3] There's something miraculous in the fact that God has sustained the Jews through multiple attempts to wipe them off the face of the earth, and the story of Esther attests to that miracle.

For Christians, the story is a reminder that God doesn't abandon his people, no matter how dark their circumstances, how compromised their hearts are, or how hidden he may seem.

Hiddenness is a theme that shapes the whole book of Esther. Mordecai and Esther have hidden identities. Haman—the story's villain—has hidden motives. More important, God himself is hidden throughout the book. His name isn't mentioned once, and his absence is a key feature of the story. God's hiddenness is what makes Esther such an important book for our day too, a day when belief in God feels always resisted, always contested, when everything seems to have a natural explanation, and when our own experience often makes us feel as though God is, indeed, absent.

Luther's charges—that it's too heathen, too scandalous—are actually part of what makes the book brilliant. Other biblical characters, like Daniel, Joseph, and the apostles in the book of Acts, all exhibit tremendous faith in the midst of a hostile environment, and God shows up in dramatic, miraculous ways. But Esther and Mordecai are far frailer, more compromised, more human. They're conflicted, out to save their skins and advance their careers or their social status. There is almost no religion in the book, only a call to fast that we can assume is also a call to prayer. So this is not a story about virtue and character, but about someone who has become acclimated to a godless world and has grown quite comfortable with it. It's about compromise and crisis, and God's way of preserving and renewing faith in the midst of it all.

When I was a kid in Sunday school, we used to sing a song called "Dare to Be a Daniel." If you understand what's happening in Esther's story, you'll never tell someone "Aspire to be an Esther."

Yet this reality brings up a final reason this story is so important for us, especially now. Because if we're honest, we do aspire to be an Esther—but for all the wrong reasons.

Esther embodies everything we think will make us happy. She is beautiful, rich, powerful; she has immense sexual charm and charisma; and she has a legion of servants at her beck and call. She's kind of the Kim Kardashian of the Old Testament.

Why is Kim Kardashian so famous? Why does she show up on magazine covers, and why do entertainment shows and websites document her every move? It's because her way of life is compelling. We think she has achieved the "good life": fame, success, money, sex, power.

Esther embodies the same life . . . right up until her spiritual crisis comes (and Esther's crisis, we'll see, is every bit as spiritual as it is political). At that point, Esther has to reckon with God and her place as one of God's people. She has to choose between power and weakness. Between safety and vulnerability. Between living a life of comfort and risking her life in hopes of saving her soul.

In the pages ahead, I'll retell the story of Esther. You'll notice that I don't quote the text much, and that's intentional. For many of us, this is a familiar story, and I want to make the familiar strange, or at least fresh. If I have taken too many liberties, I apologize. I come from a long line of storytellers, and storytellers tend to emphasize the parts they like best. Here, I am not so much trying to entertain as to bring to your attention some of the details. I also hope to help you see these characters in their glorious, broken, and sometimes terrifying humanity.

I also want to retell the story because I think it is one of the best stories in Scripture. The characters, ironies, and plot twists make the story read like an Elmore Leonard novel. And in these pages I hope that the elements of this story might surprise you a bit once again.

Most of all, I hope they give you a sense of the way forward in this strange in-between space we occupy. Whatever happens in the years and decades to come, we can be sure that faithfulness looks pretty much like it did three thousand years ago. Sometimes it looks like Daniel: a steady path of spiritual formation and obedience. But sometimes, and perhaps more often than not in the world we occupy today, it looks more like Esther: a path of awakening, risk, vulnerability, and, ultimately, hope.

CHAPTER 1

EMPIRE OF IDOLS

ACT ONE: ESTHER 1

King Xerxes was drunk. I mean, really drunk. The kind of drunk that makes everyone else at the party uncomfortable. He reeled and shouted and swung heavy arms over a crowd of onlookers and flunkies, sloshing wine and shouting about the glories of Persia.

This is where our story begins.

Some have called this drunken king "King of Kings" because his empire spread from modern-day Ethiopia to modern-day Pakistan.[1] In the book of Esther, he's called Ahasuerus (pronounced "A-hash-wer-osh"). Kings often had multiple names, which might account for why the Hebrew Bible uses this name; "Ahashwerosh" is a pun that would be heard by Hebrew speakers as "King Headache."[2] Whether the headache is from the hangover he'd have after this opening scene or from the one he'd soon cause the Jews, your guess is as good as mine.

Rule under the Persians wasn't so bad. Unlike the Assyrians, if the Persians conquered your land, they were pretty reasonable. They were deal makers; they'd leave standing kings and governors in power as long as they were willing to swear loyalty to the Persian throne, pay their share of taxes, and, from time to time, pay tribute to the Persian king. It was a protection racket: you send gold, jewels, slaves, and soldiers, and you enjoyed the knowledge that if someone else came knocking at your gates, the full fury of the Persian army would defend you.

It was the third year of his reign, and Xerxes was wrapping up a six-month-long party. He'd summoned rulers, governors, and military officials from across the empire to Susa, the wintertime capital of Persia. Aside from the lavish display of his wealth, the party was a war council, drumming up support for an upcoming campaign against the Greeks.

And so the tribute rolled in, cart after cart of livestock, wealth, oils and spices, silks and leather, gold and jewels, and slaves and concubines. The whole city rumbled with footsteps and hooves, and with the wooden drone of rolling carts.

The palace at Susa was a stunning display. The hall where the festival took place had thirty-six columns that stood seventy feet tall, each with a carving of twin bulls at the top, supporting a ceiling built with massive wooden timbers. Everything had a sculpture, an engraving, a gold embellishment, a covering of silk.

Here's how rich Xerxes was: a few years later, when the Greek war ended in failure for Persia, the Persians retreated, and the Greeks overtook their encampment, Herodotus wrote that the Greeks found gold and silver *couches* left behind.[3] Not coins. Not statues. Couches.

It's this kind of Kanye-worthy excess that Xerxes put on display for the governors. It was a display of his own wealth, and a kind of promise. A vision of their own lives, should they support their king on his next military expedition. *We'll ransack Athens, and we'll take all their stuff.* The guests drank and they feasted and they fawned over Xerxes, who got as drunk on their praise as he did on his wine.

The city itself accommodated these guests with charm, and the parties poured out into the streets as the governors, revelers, and suppliers poured in.

When the last delegation had gone home, Xerxes made a final gesture of generosity, this time to the people of Susa. Every citizen was welcomed to the palace and

treated with the same dignity and hospitality as the aristocrats who had come before them. Tanners and blacksmiths
and livestock traders sat in royal halls, heard the court
musicians, ate the food that turned on spits, and drank the
wine that was served in goblets of gold and silver. On the
walls were carvings of Xerxes as a lion, eating an antelope;
carvings of his father, Darius, telling the stories of war and
victory, painted in bright colors and brought alive by shift-
ing firelight. The commoners bathed in the godlike glory
of empire.

When the feast was announced to the city, the king
decreed, "There is no compulsion," a necessary relief for
the partiers. Normal custom would have required that anything served by the king to his guests must be consumed,
regardless of the will of the guest, the fullness of the belly,
or the level of sobriety. Instead, the king made room for
people to come and go, to drink and eat as they wished, to
enjoy his table without the burdens of decorum.

Xerxes presided over the whole thing, at times seated
on a throne above the crowd, at times mixing in with the
dazzled commoners. He drank it in with the same desperation he drank in the fawning of the royal officials. It wasn't
enough for this king to be feared; he wanted to be loved.
And the royal treasury bought innumerable casks of wine,
bushels of grain, bleating heads of sheep and goat, all to
pour out on the city like flowers from lover to beloved.
Entertainers danced and sang and told bawdy jokes day

and night. Slaves and prostitutes were put to work. To call it "excessive" is to put it mildly. One note in the Talmud, one of the principle texts of rabbinic Judaism, says that Satan himself danced among them.[4]

No matter how you frame it, the party itself was a terrifying place. The king wielded near-absolute power in his kingdom. He gave life and took it. He conscripted Susa's sons into his army and its daughters into his harem. Criminals and offenders of the crown were regularly impaled on stakes and hoisted high in the air, their twisted bodies a warning to any who thought to violate the law or fall into disfavor. His name was revered; his decrees terrified.

The citadel loomed over the city. Its gates were called the Gate to the World, because what issued from the palace shaped the world. A god lived there, and he sat on a high throne surrounded by slaves and servants and a thousand works of art that celebrated him and his divinity. And improbably, he invited them into his palace and threw them a feast.

On the seventh day of the feast, things got weird.

The king was "merry with wine" (1:10), which is a polite way to say he got drunk and stupid. The citizens of Susa were stunned by the spectacle of the "King of

Kings"—glassy-eyed and tongue-tied, staggering through a crowd of peasants.

Xerxes began shouting for the queen. He rounded up his advisors and sent them to bring her before the raging crowd.

Opinions vary on exactly what was happening at this point in the story. In some commentaries, Vashti gets painted as the villain: a stubborn wife who was too concerned with her own business to respectfully submit to her husband's request. Somewhere, there's a Sunday school teacher with polished shoes and a nice blue dress saying to a roomful of wide-eyed kids, "The nerve of that woman! Disobeying her husband?" (To be fair, this is precisely the conclusion Xerxes' council of flunkies arrived at as well.)

I have my doubts about this interpretation. After all, this was ancient Persia, meaning Vashti's summons likely would lead to some form of sexual humiliation or violence. Persia, generally speaking, was not a fun place to be a woman. Women, including the queen, were property. Vashti was wealthy and pampered, but she lived a cloistered life, surrounded by female attendants and eunuchs, subject to whatever treatment suited Xerxes at any particular moment. She likely wasn't a friend and companion. She was certainly not a ruler or dignitary, as we might imagine a queen to be.

It was never safe to be a woman in Persia, and on a

night when the king and his attendants were drunk with wine and the promise of war, it was the least safe of all.

Even the queen and her attendants might not be spared from public humiliation. At a minimum, Xerxes' request would have required some kind of display. He might have wanted Vashti to emerge in the hall wearing only a crown, or perhaps a crown and an open robe, her beauty silencing the bands, filling the drunken mass with lust. It might have been far worse.

But not tonight. She heard the throb of the music, the roar of the mob. And tonight, Vashti would say no. For her dignity. For the dignity of her handmaidens. For the women of Persia, Vashti would say no. And no one said no to the king when the king was "God."

And yet, in the presence of the ordinary people of Susa, when the king, plastered and shameless, shouted for the queen, she *did* say no. The king was humiliated—and shellacked.

When the hangovers were cured and the halls were quiet again, a long counsel was taken with the king and his advisors. Queen Vashti had set a dangerous precedent.

"What if women begin refusing their husbands' demands?"

"They might begin thinking and acting for themselves!"

"Even our own wives might be emboldened against us!"

"Something must be done!"

One of the advisors proposed a solution: Banish Vashti. Make an example of her. Show the women of Persia that there were consequences for disrespecting their husbands. This would settle a thousand domestic disputes and keep women from getting any high-minded ideas about what they could learn from Vashti.

Hidden in this suggestion was another thought: *the men of Persia will love you for this.*

And so it was done. Letters went out to all of the empire, warning the women of Persia, announcing that for her insolence, Vashti was no longer queen and was banished forever. It was the first step in a story that would pitch the empire into turmoil and would push the Jews living in Persia right up to the edge of genocide.

A WORLD MUCH LIKE OUR OWN

At first glance, it's tempting to look at ancient Persia as a world so unlike our own as to be incomprehensible. Primitive people. Primitive society. Primitive technology and religion and ideas about humanity, nothing at all like us. To think this is understandable. But doing so is a huge mistake.

Generally speaking, the human heart hasn't changed much in the last few thousand years. People are people, each one subject to passions, fears, and insecurities. The interior life of an ancient Persian dictator or an Assyrian goat herder was not terribly unlike your own.

In his documentary *The Cave of Forgotten Dreams*, Werner Herzog explores ancient cave drawings that were discovered in France. The drawings are elegant, depicting animals in motion along the cave wall. Water runs through the caves too, and Herzog shows how light from fire and torches reflects off the moving water and onto the walls, shimmering through the drawings and animating them. Watching the light move along the images, you realize that humanity at its most primitive had imaginations, like you and I, possessed a love for beauty, and—in all likelihood—shared a propensity to gaze at images and tell stories. They had charcoal sketches of deer and bulls. We have Netflix. But the life of the mind is no different.

The same thing goes for Persian relief carvings, statuary, architecture, and mythology. Their culture reflects the hungers of the human heart, much as our own does.

When we look at Persia through that lens, we see much that is familiar. We see Xerxes' architectural achievements and military power—his sprawling palaces that reflected his sprawling empire. The display was both political and personal. A hunger for love and fear that centers not only in a longing for loyalty to the empire, but to the king himself. Xerxes was mortal. He had a soul, like you and I, and in our fallen world, our hearts are always desperate to make sense of who we are, to discover whether or not we matter. We all build empires in hopes of inspiring love, loyalty, and admiration. Some just have the ability to do it on a grander scale than others.

So Xerxes paraded before the world all of those things that—for all of human history—have held out the promise of happiness. Money. Power. Sex. His table, his treasury, and his harem were overflowing, and he wanted the world to see it and stand in awe.

The feast was also part of Persia's program for assimilation. Empires existed because one ruler was able, through political and military means, to assimilate many kingdoms and peoples under one banner. For peace to exist in the empire, you didn't just need strength; you needed a certain kind of love and loyalty. If you were Xerxes, you'd want to find ways to get people who might otherwise prefer self-government to think, *It sure is great to be a Persian.* Showering rulers and governors with overabundance at a feast goes a long way toward that goal.

Another way you do this—which will become important soon—is by assimilating their religions. Like the Babylonians before them, the Persians embraced a certain pragmatism when it came to religion. In many ancient empires, the conquering culture would demand a religious overhaul of the conquered, exchanging their sun god for the empire's lizard god or whatever. The Persians and the Babylonians did things a little differently. You were welcome to keep your sun god or your lizard god, so long as you saw that god as part of the broader pantheon of gods of that empire. This worked well, with a few exceptions (the Jews being one of them).

And here, too, our world and Esther's world overlap. The truly dangerous idea in Persia and Babylon (and the only real heresy) was to believe that *your* religion was the one true religion.

It disturbed the tidy order of things. It made for religious dissidents, and it caused friction amid polite pluralism. In our world, the same is true, although for different reasons. Where their world was overtly pagan, ours wears a mask of secularism.

THE PROBLEM WITH PLURALISM

Religion as a rigid worldview and lifestyle-shaping force has been largely denigrated into a series of entrees from a restaurant menu. Two hundred years ago, if you were born Catholic or Hindu or Muslim, it was almost impossible to convert to another religion without causing serious social upheaval. It happened, but it wasn't normal. Now, in the Western world, people can generally believe whatever they want, or they can believe in nothing, and it's all acceptable.

The one thing that isn't quite acceptable is holding to some kind of exclusive belief. Christians, Jews, and Muslims who believe their religion is right to the exclusion of others are facing increasing cultural pressure and hostility.

But religion hasn't disappeared entirely. People spend thousands of dollars on transcendental meditation retreats, and that practice (as well as mindfulness meditation) has advocates in academia and the business world. And while they'd never identify themselves as religions, there are movements and elements in our secular culture that are religious, like it or not. These movements and their adherents promise hidden knowledge, happiness, or moral virtue: vegans, home birthers, anti-vaxxers, homeopathic medicine, or any one of a dozen food orthodoxies. I mention them not to condemn them but to highlight the passion that each can inspire. Similarly, there's an almost religious fanaticism that hooks people on activities such as CrossFit, SoulCycle, or yoga. We're creatures looking for meaning and purpose, and these pursuits can quickly become pseudo-religions that offer some sense of meaning or a hint of longed-for transcendence.

There are streams of religion that survive in this world, but they only thrive if they're treated with the same casual air as, say, SoulCycle and yoga. They're fine, so long as you don't take them too seriously. They shouldn't be the North Star around which you (much less "we") should organize our lives. Instead, religions and various forms of spirituality are treated like items on a buffet, to be taken or left however your appetites dictate.

Trouble only brews if you dare suggest that someone else's practice isn't as good as yours. Doing so disrupts the happy, pluralistic world, and it sets one citizen against the others.

Mostly, these disruptions happen on Facebook. And when things blow up there, it's generally harmless. Say a few parents start duking it out over vaccines or milk with hormones in it: Those battles usually end with someone saying, "Look, everyone needs to do what's right for their family," a platitude that sends everyone back into their collective corners. And even when that doesn't work, the worst thing that happens is someone unfriends somebody, and relative peace ensues again.

That's why these religions tend to thrive: They're mostly

harmless. Their goals are narcissistic, me-centered. They don't make demands on society, on neighbors, or even on families. In this, they're like temples to the sun god or the lizard god. Let the people offer up blood sacrifices or sexual sacrifices or whatever it is they do, as long as they're not intent on destroying one another and—here's the real kicker—so long as they acknowledge that Xerxes or Caesar or Nebuchadnezzar is a god too. And because he's the king, he's actually the one god that matters. The one they need to fear the most. Which brings me back to secularism.

THE ONE GOD THAT MATTERS TODAY

Secularism is today's incontestable god. It's the one that oversees the way the other gods function in our society. Because while it hasn't erased religion or spirituality, it has created a backdrop that leaves it always secondary. The bedrock ideas of our world say that all that exists is what can be seen, touched, tasted, smelled, and comprehended through ordinary means. So, for instance, secularism denies real transcendence. It might allow for the possibility of the *experience* of transcendence, but it must explain it via these material causes: What we call transcendence or religious experience is actually some combination of good hormones and happy neurons in the brain. It has some evolutionary cause—some root in the need to advance and preserve our species that has been written into our DNA.

Secularists can tolerate religion as long as it doesn't make claims on anyone else's happiness or welfare—that is, as long as it doesn't purport to be an all-inclusive picture of the good life. So, when religion or spirituality are mostly self-serving, when it doesn't make demands of anyone but its acolytes, secularism leaves room for it. "Do your transcendental meditation retreat. Eat your tofurky," it says. "Just don't try to assign any big, overarching meaning to them. Don't let them frame up the whole world. Don't let your beliefs cast aspersion on your neighbors, and most of all, don't let them compete with *me*."

In Persia, Babylon, and Rome, people who didn't buy into pluralism ran into trouble. They found themselves oppressed or isolated, or trampled by Xerxes' elephants. Something similar is happening to Christians today.

To stretch the metaphor, let's imagine that a group that had been deliberately picking fights with Xerxes, outlawing Xerxes-related paraphernalia in their towns and villages and refusing to do business with Persians, conducted some raids along the Christian/Persian border. Their resistance might have worked for a while. They might have won a few battles with Persian troops, and they may have even thought they'd won self-rule back. But the reach of the empire and the momentum of its growth were too great. Eventually, they would have to either assimilate, shrink into ghettos, or perish.

For a long time, Christians were gleeful combatants in the culture wars. They occupied a place of power. Though they saw that power beginning to shift in the aftermath of the 1960s and '70s, they thought they could legislate and enforce a hard line against it. But eventually, they lost, and their opponents turned their tactics against them. Which is where we are now. There's a big, decadent, secularist feast going on.

What Christians underestimated, or perhaps simply didn't see coming, was how much momentum secularism had, and how powerfully it would impact the human imagination. Secularism tells us that the universe is comprehensible, and that's a dazzling thought. All mysteries have solutions. Copernicus showed us how the stars moved, and that we weren't in the center of them. Darwin showed us how humanity came into being. Freud said that the voice in your head wasn't an evil spirit; it was your mother.

These ideas and others layered on top of one another, eventually untethering the world from any thoughts about God, and with them, any ideas about real authority. Secularism unleashes humanity to a life of (supposed) autonomous human freedom, freeing it to seek out pleasure and happiness wherever they're found, freeing it from the burden of arbitrary laws from an angry, bearded giant in the sky.

In this reframed world, even nature loses any real sense of authority. What we might call "interventions" into nature become commonplace, whether we're talking about splitting the atom, enhancing breasts, or calling a biological male a woman. I don't mean to draw an equivalence among these things, only to point out that in each case, something happens that is wholly unnatural. In a world without God or without authority, we have few resources for thinking about and judging the merits of any of these. They each come down to—at best—a question of "the good of the many" and "the good of the few." Culture, as a whole, has reasoned that a host of things are acceptable paths to happiness, from gay marriage to polyamory and more. Who are you to object to someone else's chosen path?

SEARCHING FOR MEANING

Another aspect of life in a secular age is its frenzied consumerism. In a world without God, life remains a quest for satisfaction and meaning, and marketers have learned to prey on our insecurities and longings in hopes of stirring an appetite for their products. To live in the midst of such a culture is to be subject to a thousand little acts of violence and hostility. Watching even a half hour of television will subject you to a dozen displays of inadequacy: You're too old, too ugly, too busy, not busy enough, too poor, too dull, too sad—but don't worry! We have a product for sale that can solve your problems.

Behind each of these insults is some enthroned ideal, some vision for life that holds out the promise of happiness. It may be youth or beauty; it may be some imagined familial Eden, where children are healthy and well-adjusted after years of proper parenting; it may be the promise of wealth or fame or that obnoxious buzzword *influence*. And each of these ideals has a face, a celebrity endorser whose life embodies the life we think would make us happy. We buy the products they endorse. We wear their brands. We attend their seminars and read their books. We lay down our cash and sacrifice our time in hopes that they'll give us what they've promised: some measure of peace, some foretaste of utopia. Like the Persians, we have our temples and we have our pantheon of little gods.

Don't mishear me though. I don't hold these out with the intent to shame you, dear reader. Instead, I want to play the part of Toto, sneaking behind the Wizard's curtain to reveal the disappointing ordinariness of these idols, and to unveil the reality that they're quite incapable of helping us.

More than that, I want to point to the *hunger* that drives us to them. Some of that hunger is as old as the events that unfold in Genesis 3. It's the homesickness of exiled humanity, longing to get back to the satisfying, peace-filled world we were made for. That hunger intensifies in a culture that thrives on stoking it, and stoking our hunger means inflicting wounds. It's in the interest of our idols—and in the interest of those who profit from our idol worship—to make sure we are feeling small, defeated, depressed, and inadequate. It makes it far easier to separate from our money. Something in the shadows stokes a sorrow in our bellies, preys on our homesick longings, and sends us off to the temples in search of help.

We live in the shadow of idols who have what we want, who promise to heal us if we worship them, and who always disappoint. We enthrone power, wealth, and sexuality, and these gods inflict a thousand traumas on us by preying on our inadequacy.

We can't dismiss the backdrop of Esther's world; it is far more like our own than we—the enlightened, with our smartphones and our mythless secularity—would like to believe. The idols have changed their clothes, but they remain as vicious as ever.

SHAPING OUR DESIRES

One clear example may be found in idols related to sexuality and, in particular, how these idols shape the way both cultures treat women. In Persia, women were essentially property, and while we can certainly acknowledge that women's place in society has been improved, we shouldn't feel *too* self-righteous.

It's no wonder that shortly after secularism took hold of the popular imagination, we saw the rise of what journalist Pamela Paul has designated a "pornified"[5] culture, where women seem to be more objectified than ever before. Pornography seeks to tap into our most base desires and sell them back to us. And as Paul describes in her book, porn has a progressive quality. The appetite grows larger, and the consumer spirals into consuming darker and more violent stuff.

We also have a hookup culture that divorces sex from relationships. We have apps such as Tinder that make hooking up feel like playing a video game. The lines of what is and isn't sex have shifted for many young people, as have the norms that dictate at what age sexual activity should begin and how serious any sexual relationship should be.

Now, there's an argument that says that all of this is progress.

"Women are liberated from oppressive sexuality like ancient Persia's. They're free to do what they want to do. So, if they want to make porn and go from hookup to hookup, then more power to them." But when we say that, we automatically assume that what people *want* is a matter of their own free will.

We like to think of ourselves as autonomous actors in the world. We think our desires are innate; they're *ours*, and what we want is something that has developed freely and independently.

But our desires don't appear out of nowhere, innate to our hearts. Rather, they're formed by innumerable explicit and implicit influences that range from our family system to our education to media to politics. When God tells us that we're clay, it's not just a happy image that promises that he—the Potter— has the power to shape us. It means that we are moldable, and *something is always forming and shaping us.* Our culture tells stories that shape what we think is good and what might make us happy, and our hearts conform to those stories.[6]

This is how most of our desires work: Through cultural stories, we're offered images of the good life: pathways to love, romance, sexual fulfillment, power, money, and happiness. These stories grab hold of our hearts, and they shape what we think we want.[7]

Thus, women participate in a culture that objectifies and devalues them with a false sense of liberation. They're free to do what they want, so they can sext with loser boyfriends and make porn and enjoy a long string of casual hookups. But we must ask whether what they *want* to do has been shaped by the culture around them, whether they've been coerced into thinking that these things are good, normal pathways to happiness. We must then ask if our world is valuing women or deceiving them into a false sense of freedom, making them willing participants in a culture that objectifies and abuses them.

In this way, we are no different from the Persians. While the Persians codified their misogyny in explicit traditions and laws, we enforce ours more subtly, through media and entertainment. In both worlds, women learn to live as objects, and it becomes difficult to imagine another way of being. Female empowerment and objectification seem to go hand in hand, and most of our culture's examples of "powerful women" are celebrities who embrace some degree of explicit sexuality or objectification.

This illustrates how idols work. Like any god, the idol of sex makes a promise and demands a sacrifice. It promises fulfillment and satisfaction, yet comes with a cost. In Persia, the dignity of women was sacrificed for the pleasure of men. In our day, when women are shaped and formed by a culture that tells them they must fulfill roles modeled by actresses, pop stars, and supermodels, where their bodies are meant for display, how are we any different?

In both worlds, sex is unhinged from its purposes in creation. It has lost its roots in fidelity, family, procreation, and spirituality. The body itself has primarily become a vessel for pleasure, and sex becomes increasingly frenzied and destructive.

As with all idols, we've tapped into something good and stretched it beyond its purpose and value. Or perhaps it's better to say that we've made something glorious into something petty, turning the spiritual wonder and mystery of sexual union into a simple appetite and a meaningless encounter.

Here's another way to think about it: The book of Ecclesiastes says that humanity has eternity in its heart (3:11). I take this to mean that our longing for eternity, for experiencing the transcendent, the beautiful, or the numinous, is ingrained and somewhat irresistible. Likewise, the Bible presents a vision of sexuality that is profoundly spiritual. Sex unites bodies and souls, whether you believe that or not, and thus it's always a way of making contact with the spiritual and eternal. In a world drained of transcendence, sex is a powerful outlier. We might rationally deny that it means anything, but the experience it offers scratches a more-than-physical itch. We were made to relish the spiritual and physical pleasures of sex, and when we're starved for spiritual experience, that particular outlet is going to be all the more powerful—and it's as powerful now as it was in Persia.

WELCOME TO DYSTOPIA

Of course, sex is just one example among many. Sex rises to obscene extremes along with all kinds of consumption. It's an awful lot like *The Hunger Games*, where the outlying districts sacrifice and labor to satisfy the decadent urges of the Capitol. But *The Hunger Games* isn't just a dystopian vision of the future; it's a vision of our present: disdain for human life, unconstrained consumption, and the spiritual poverty of secularism. Again: if existence is just a big cosmic accident, then what's to constrain our consumption? Why not eat till we vomit and then eat some more? Why not push pleasure-seeking and sexuality to their very extremes? Why not please and satisfy ourselves on the backs of the unprivileged masses who make it possible?

Occasionally, someone rises up and says, "Maybe all of this isn't such a good idea." She resists the objectification—and she pays the price for it. This, I believe, is what happened to Vashti. I'm surprised she wasn't killed for it.

Esther 1 ends with Xerxes reminding the empire that women are subservient to men. A secular age accomplishes something similar—divorcing sex from anything meaningful, creating the illusion of autonomy, and immersing women in a world that talks a good feminist game while consistently objectifying women and training them to be taken advantage of by men. One is overt. The other is subversive. Both result in coercive and dehumanizing cultures that operate in service to an idol.

The message of Esther 1 is clear: Those who might resist the status quo are put on notice. Your dissent is not welcome. Your refusal to participate will result in exile.

Here again is a parallel between Esther's world and our own. As society's norms increasingly become a sexual free-for-all, voices of dissent have become increasingly unwelcome. And while we're yet to see anyone shipping Christians off into exile, there are consequences for those who resist. They are labeled "intolerant," called bigots, made unwelcome in media, academia, and the marketplace. At times, they're subjected to lawsuits over flowers, pizza, and wedding cakes. Resistance is dangerous, and while it may not get you shipped off into a literal exile, it can certainly lead to a social one.

CHAPTER 2

CONQUEST AND COMPROMISE

ACT TWO: ESTHER 2:1-5

Vashti's insubordination toward Xerxes was the first in a series of unfortunate events.

In the months after, Xerxes marched to war with the full weight of the Persian army. His father, Darius, had been humiliated by the Greeks, and Xerxes' campaign was a bloodthirsty quest for revenge.

But it wasn't to be.

It's a famous war, perhaps most famous for the Battle of Thermopylae. On the road to Athens sat a narrow pass, and several thousand Greeks were sent to block the Persian army. Herodotus, a historian of roughly the same era, said the Persians sent as many as five million. This is probably an exaggeration, designed to highlight the superiority of the Greek forces over the Persians, and is a reminder that the victors write the history books. Nevertheless, it seems safe to say that the Greeks were vastly outnumbered.

The standoff in the pass lasted seven days. At some point, the Greeks were betrayed, and the Persians were shown a narrow workaround for the pass, which would allow them to send forces to attack from the rear. A Spartan general learned of the betrayal and sent most of the Greeks home, leaving a small force of a few hundred Thespians and Thebans, and, of course, the famous "300"—the Spartan warriors, known to be the fiercest and most fearless. This small force held off the Persians (ostensibly "millions" of them) for days, and though they were eventually annihilated, their stand allowed the Greeks to assemble forces and ready for war.

The war went on for about two years, and Athens burned. But eventually, the Greeks repelled the Persians. The Persian army was ill-equipped for the fight against the Greeks. They were armed with bows and arrows, light armor, and weapons meant for hand-to-hand combat. Some of them only wore leather tunics and fought with spears tipped with antlers. Their strategy was to shower an opposing force with a brutal hailstorm of arrows (some accounts said their volleys of arrows could black out the sun) and to clean up whoever was left with overwhelming numbers attacking in a melee.

They had been quite effective throughout the empire, and the world feared them. But the Greeks had superior armor and, more important, superior tactics. The Greek soldiers—called "hoplites"—stood shoulder to shoulder in battle, each armed with a massive shield and a long spear. Their formation was called a *phalanx*, and it was nearly impenetrable; they could shield themselves from the onslaught of arrows and still stab anything that came near them. The phalanx is what held back the Persians at Thermopylae, and eventually, repelled the Persians altogether from Europe.

Xerxes came home defeated, driven back by smaller, but smarter, armies. And it is this Xerxes—beaten, embittered, humiliated—that we find in Esther 2.

What was a defeated god to do? How should a tyrant respond when his wealth and stature are terribly diminished . . . but not so diminished as to render him powerless?

Xerxes brooded and sulked and stormed through the palace. He handed out harsh punishments as a way of soothing his shattered ego. Not content with his harem, he seduced the wives and daughters of the aristocrats around him. He drank. He feasted. He grew fatter, angrier. Rather than shower his governors with excess, as he had in the past, he consumed it himself, drowning his sorrows by feeding his most primitive urges. He nursed grudges and dreamed of war, but faced daily the failure of planning, failure of strategy, failure of strength, and failure of nerve that had sent him home from Greece empty-handed.

The palace walked on eggshells. The king's advisors plotted various ways to renew the king's strength and focus, or at least to distract him from his bitterness. Finally, one day, someone said, "I've got it."

"A new queen?" asked the king.

"A new queen," answered the advisor. He stood with the other governors in the towering, empty throne room.

There's a midrash—a Jewish commentary on the story—that says that Xerxes had been drunk when he made the decree to banish Vashti. When he sobered up, the story goes, he beheaded the advisors who had suggested it. If that version of the story is true, then Xerxes was a fool who loved Vashti but couldn't constrain his temper.

In any case, Vashti's banishment still hung like a shadow over the palace. Yes, the king had made his point, and yes, the order of things in Persia had been restored by banishing the queen for disobeying her husband. But nonetheless, Xerxes looked weak.

He was frustrated to be without her, whether it was because of the emptiness of her throne, or the emptiness of his heart. (Given the size of a Persian king's harem, we can be sure it was not the emptiness of his bed.)

"What if," said the advisor, "you could have your pick from every beautiful young girl in Persia?"

"I think that's a given," responded the king.

"No . . . I mean . . . we bring them *all* here, and you have them one by one until you find one that you think should be queen."

Xerxes sat back. He scratched his chin. The mechanics of the plan turned over in his mind. It was the exact opposite of Vashti's banishment. She had refused him and was sent away. Here, none could refuse without facing the wrath of the empire, and all of these girls would become part of his collection. It was a revenge of sorts, not on Vashti herself, but on the kingdom. On any who dared laugh at Vashti's defiance of the king. On any who doubted his power after Greece.

It would be more than a feast for his greedy lust and his inner emptiness. It was a terror campaign, equivalent in many respects to the campaigns of Herod and Pharaoh to wipe out a generation of firstborn sons. In this case, these girls would be stripped from their homes, subjected to systematic rape, and locked away afterward, never to be known by another man, never to raise a family, never to know a normal life again. By law, no one who'd been with the king could ever know another man. Philosopher Yoram Hazony noted how appealing this was to the king's fragile, shattered ego. The king would never fear that "another in the kingdom [would] be told in the dead of some night, years hence, that he was a better man than the king, for she [would] have no other man."[1]

On the surface, the story might look a little like *The Bachelor: Ancient Persia*. It's more like *Who Wants to Marry a Brutal Persian Dictator?* It's a story of kidnapping, human trafficking, and rape. Some might go willingly, ready to participate in the competition for the throne. But for most, the decree was tyrannical. It was an act of conquest that Xerxes most certainly wouldn't lose.

It is here, in our story, that we come to meet Mordecai. The scripture reads, "Now there was a Jew in Susa the citadel whose name was Mordecai" (2:5). For modern readers, that sentence holds no big surprises. But for its original Jewish audience, it made their ears hurt.

We know the name Mordecai as a Jewish name. But it isn't originally Jewish—it was embraced by Jews *because* of this one. Mordecai is actually a Persian name, and worse than that, it's a name that honors the Persian god Marduk. Again, we might not be able to appreciate what a big deal this is. But let's glance back a few pages to the book of Nehemiah, where the prophet returns to Jerusalem to find that Jews have intermarried with non-Jews and are raising their kids to speak languages other than Hebrew. It isn't a pretty scene. The prophet drags people out into the street and beats them for such an offense. Imagine how incensed he'd be to find out they'd been naming their children after foreign gods.

To be a Jew, first and foremost, is to be called out and set apart from the rest of the world. In the Old Testament, everything important about being Jewish—dietary laws, practicing the Sabbath, declaring "The LORD our God . . . is one"—made them distinct from their non-Jewish neighbors (Deut. 6:4). And so the phrase *a Jew in Susa named Mordecai* is scandalous.

It brings to mind the Jewish comedian Jackie Mason's joke: "In the United States nobody has a Jewish name. Americans want to make sure they don't sound too Jewish, so every Jewish kid now is Tiffany Schwartz. Allison Ginsburg. Ashley Lipshitz. . . . I know one kid that's named Crucifix Finkelstein."[2]

A Jew named Mordecai is a bit like a Jew named "Crucifix Finkelstein."

Mordecai's name isn't the only thing that makes his introduction startling. Read it again: "There was a Jew in Susa the citadel." Not Susa the city, which wrapped around the citadel, where the Jewish exiles would have lived, but in the citadel itself, at the heart of Persian power and politics.

It'd be one thing if his name was Abraham or David and he lived in the citadel, we'd have reason to suspect he hadn't compromised his Jewish identity. Likewise, it might be forgivable to be named Mordecai and live among the Jewish exiles in the city of Susa. But a Jew named Mordecai living in the citadel was a compromised person. He'd sacrificed his identity and taken up a place in the center of power in a foreign government—a government that had been more gracious, perhaps, than the Babylonians toward the Jews, but a foreign government with a demigod king and a pagan religion at its core.

There should be no doubt about it when we meet Mordecai: he's a compromised man, living with a Persian identity in service to a Persian king.

THE PATH TO EXILE

We have to back up a bit. We need to sketch in a few details. We'll start with kings. Not the book of Kings—the idea of kings. The Bible isn't fond of them.

The patriarch Abraham had come out of Ur. He was probably something like an aristocrat: a wealthy landowner, perhaps a warlord, or perhaps part of the royal family. Whatever the case, he was heirless, and when God called him out of Ur and promised him an heir, he exchanged a way of life that was part of a human hierarchal order for one that was mystical. God was his King, and where God sent him, he'd go.

Fast-forward to Israel post-exodus. Like Abraham, the Israelites followed God as their King, and where he said to go, they'd go. They had a prophet who led them, and he appointed a council of elders to provide some order for the community, but they had no king. Their first king didn't come along until after many years of failure and judgment—and then only because they begged God for it.

"You're not going to like it," God warned them.

"But everyone around us has a king, and he keeps them safe!" Israel said.

"You're really not going to like it," God repeated. "Besides, I, God, am your King. Who could be a better king than God?"

"But a human king would keep us in line, and you wouldn't have to send judges to straighten us out and call us back to faithfulness," Israel argued.

"Okay . . . if you insist," God agreed, and he gave them a king named Saul.

That didn't work out so well. Saul was temperamental, insecure, and egotistic. His rash judgment endangered the lives of those around him and the safety of the kingdom.

Next came David, and he was, for the most part, the king Israel longed for. A hero. A warrior. A faithful worshipper. He was also an adulterer and a murderer, but everyone has their flaws. At the least, you have to give him credit for being a faithful worshipper and a guy who could repent of his sins. No one's done it better since Psalm 51.

There was a great deal of squabbling about whom David's heir would be, but eventually came Solomon, and Solomon managed to finish the temple in Jerusalem and usher in one of the most peaceful and prosperous seasons in the history of the Jews. He also had his flaws. He seemed to love concubines, wine, food, and fancy clothes a bit too much, but hey—the temple, right?

After Solomon, things started to decline faster and faster. The nation seesawed between faithfulness and failure. One king built Asherah poles and started worshiping fertility gods. The next one found the Torah buried in a pile of rubble and led the nation in repentance. The Philistines came and went, as did the prophets of Baal. Israel's trajectory was steadily downward.

Eventually, a prophet came along, warning them that the kingdom's days were numbered. The Babylonians were coming, and through them, God would punish the whole kingdom for their sins.

LAW, OBEDIENCE, AND "THE GOOD LIFE"

Sometimes the God of the Old Testament gets a bad rap, often for things like these prophecies of doom. The Babylonian exile and the destruction of Jerusalem was a really dark time in the life of God's people. We tend to ask *why* a lot around stories like this: Why didn't God protect them? Why didn't he raise up better prophets and give Israel softer hearts? Why didn't he give the Babylonians hemorrhoids, like he did the Philistines? (Not joking: see 1 Samuel 5 in the Darby Translation or the Jubilee Bible.)

The answer is twofold. The first is to point to the mystery of God's providence. No one knows why God does what he does until he tells them, and anyone who says otherwise is probably trying to sell you something. This includes the darkest moments in human history, from natural disasters to war to the events in the book of Esther. To say God takes pleasure in them is a lie— it's simply not in his character ("I take no pleasure in the death of the wicked," Ezek. 33:11; "God is not tempted by evil," James 1:13, CSB both). But it's also a lie to say that God is powerless to stop them.

Here we arrive at a timeless mystery. The tension in the midst of God's love, God's power, and the presence of evil in the world has burdened believers for thousands of years. Most of humanity has seen it as a riddle to solve—this was the approach of Job and his friends (an approach that notably failed). If it's a *mystery* and not a *riddle*, then it's something we behold and entrust to God. As much as it may trouble and confuse us, it's not confusing or troubling to God, and our burden is to trust him to sort things out while we await his promise to ultimately reconcile it all in Jesus.

When we encounter terror in the world—be it conquering empires, political crises, or the brutal kidnap-and-rape campaign of Xerxes—we have every reason to resist it, in hope that God will work through our efforts to end it. Should our efforts fail, though, we can trust that God, for reasons of his own, will work his will—whether or not we understand what that is—through the circumstances.

The second answer to the "why" question, at least in how it relates to Israel, has to do with obedience, disobedience, and consequences. Israel had a mandate from God to be a holy, set-apart nation through which he'd reveal his glory to the whole world. Central to that mandate was the law, given through Moses, which outlined an entire way of life for the Jewish people. It came as they made their way to the promised land, and it was meant to form them as a society in a way that ran counter to their soon-to-be neighbors in Canaan. As Eugene Peterson has described it, the law prepared Israel to be:

> Dumped into the moral chaos of pagan Canaanite culture, a cesspool of vile customs and sexual promiscuity. The Hebrews needed guidelines on fundamental, everyday issues of diet and nutrition, hygiene and diseases, agriculture and animals, sex and other aspects of moral behavior. Maybe most of all they needed worship rituals that would keep them attentive to God's preservation and forgiveness in their everyday lives, a sacrificial system that would replace the abhorrent child-burning sacrifices to the god Molech.[3]

I love Peterson's description of the law here. The law was not simply restrictive, but constructive; it formed the Israelites as a people and set them apart.

Yet most of the time when we talk about the law, it's in the negative. It feels strange and excessive to us, rules about shellfish and cooking. It's full of phrases like, "Don't cook a goat in the milk of its mother," "Anyone who has sex with an animal shall be put to death," and "Cut off her hand and show her no pity" (Ex. 22:19; 23:19; 34:26; Lev. 20:15; Deut. 14:21; 25:12, author's translations). It's a bloody business, this law.

But there's another way to think about it, and it helps to frame *why* Israel collapsed and *how*. Upon first examination, most people look at the law and see the Ten Commandments as the easy ones and the dietary laws as the hard ones. It's relatively easy to keep from murder; it's hard to remember which animals are off-limits, which days we can sow grain, and when sex is allowed with your own spouse and when it isn't. But this is exactly wrong. It's actually easy to not eat shrimp when you know it puts you on the outs with God. The hard part is not murdering someone.

Imagine a scenario. You go to dinner at your aunt Helen's house. She serves up a fabulous shrimp étouffée and a jambalaya with crawfish. She also has some French bread and a nice salad. If you had committed to the dietary laws, you'd find it easy in that moment to remember that eating this food will put you on the outs with God. So you eat bread and salad and you kiss Aunt Helen and insist that she's a fabulous host in spite of forgetting that you're supposed to eat kosher.

But then you drive home and discover your wife in bed with your best friend. You feel the blind rage of betrayal, both from your spouse and your so-called friend. And that blind rage makes you want to pick him up by the neck and toss him out a second-story window.

That's the real temptation of the evening, not the shrimp.

The Ten Commandments are actually the hard ones because they inhibit us at our most desperate moments. Theft sometimes comes from greed, but it also comes from need. Adultery sometimes comes from lust, but it also comes from profound loneliness. Murder comes sometimes from a cold disregard for human life, but it also stems from blind rage.

Take Xerxes himself: In the aftermath of his Greek failures and his shattered ego, it would have been easy for him to obey a few ceremonial rules and participate in obligatory religious rites. In fact, he almost certainly did. The hard thing would have been to restrain his sorrow so it didn't turn to fury, or to restrain his fury so it didn't turn to soul-crushing violence, wrought upon the very people who had sacrificed to make his failed efforts possible.

The law isn't just a restriction; it's a signpost. It cries out against great evil because it's *better*—for your soul and for society—not to throw your friend out the window. It's *better* not to steal when you're hungry. It's *better* to seek contentment than to foster envy. Doing so makes for a better life, a better society. It's a picture of the good life.

Jesus told the elderly apostle John that it was better to be hot or cold than to be lukewarm. Israel under the reign of kings was decidedly lukewarm. Their seesawing between faithfulness and idolatry meant they had a foot in both worlds—some of the moralism and restraint of the law, and some of the power-seeking of idolatry. And that, I suspect, is part of what made them vulnerable to the Philistines, the prophets of Baal, and the Babylonians.

The same thing applies to believers in all times and in all places. When God's people face opposition, including the cultural opposition Christians face today from a post-Christian world, the path of least resistance is the path of compromise. It's a foot in both worlds. *I'll give you an ethical compromise here so long as you let me speak of faith in public.* But if history teaches anything, these compromises always end in weakening the church's prophetic witness. See, for instance, the accommodations made by the church in World War II–era Germany or the accommodations of the church in the South to slavery. Not only did they do little to nothing to slow the progress of genocide or stop people from treating human beings as livestock, they also burned down the integrity of their witness for generations to come.

EXILE AND IDENTITY

The time came when Israel was weakened enough to not only lose battles, but to lose a war, and the Babylonians came in and sacked Jerusalem. When they did, they took about ten thousand of the city's elites back to Babylon, to begin to assimilate them into society. It's a smart strategy; if you can turn politicians, clerics, academics, and artisans into good, pluralistic Babylonians, you can reshape the contours of Jewish life.

This is the point where not only the Ten Commandments but the rest of the law becomes most important. Armed with it, the exiles had a way of life that could sustain their separate identity in the midst of another culture.

That's why the strange laws of the Torah had so much value for the exiles. It made the Jews into weirdos who didn't eat shrimp, ordered their steaks well done, and wouldn't taste a beef stew if there was a little cream in it. God calls this "holi-ness" because to be holy is to be set apart, and in the case of the Jewish exiles—especially Daniel and his friends—they *were* set apart. They were obviously Jewish, and their resistance to conformity got them thrown into ovens and dropped into pits with lions.

And as much as we like to pooh-pooh these things today, something similar exists in our context. We don't treat it as law, per se, but rules that govern food, dress, and relationships are still what define our communal borders. These aren't small preferences—like what movies we enjoy—but the prejudices of the big cultural tribes that we tend to sort ourselves into.[4] We not only belong to a group, but we feel a burden to project that sense of identity into the world. Some people call this "tribal sig-naling." Philosopher Charles Taylor calls it "mutual display."[5] It's evident in the fact that, generally speaking, people live most of their lives surrounded by people who look, think, and act much like them. Conservative Christians tend to spend most of their time around conservative Christians. Progressives spend their time with progressives.

In the New Testament, this kind of communal identity became a problem. Gentiles got "grafted in" to Abraham's fam-ily tree, and it became imperative that these communal borders break down so that no one was left out. There was no Greek or Jew or slave or free man who was exempt. Everyone held every-thing in common. The social order around race, gender, and poverty had to be broken down so everyone was made welcome in the church. This wasn't easy. In Acts 6, conflict emerged when concerns were raised about equality between Hellenistic Jews and Hebraic Jews. A special committee had to be formed to oversee food distribution and ensure that everyone was receiving equal treatment.

In his first letter to the Corinthians, Paul commanded women in the church to wear head coverings—a command that often gets read as a sign of the Bible's unfair treatment of women. In actuality the Corinthian church was a diverse mix of rich and poor converts, some of whom had long hair (a sign of wealth and privilege), some of whom had sold their hair, and some of whom had shaved heads (a necessary part of their work as pagan temple prostitutes). Rich, poor, or bald, all would gather with their heads covered as a symbol of their equal status under Christ and as a sign of solidarity with their sisters in Christ (11:4–10).

Unity in the church wasn't easy; it demanded leadership, submission to one another, and a willingness to put away one's privilege—rich women covered their heads and rich families weren't given special seats. And of course, this isn't easy now. Most of us attend churches where everyone looks, thinks, and acts just like us. Sunday morning, as has often been pointed out, is the most racially segregated hour of the week. I would add that it's socioeconomically segregated as well.

This is the opposite of what the New Testament holds up as its ideal. Rather than an ethnically and culturally bonded community, the church's bond is to be around the gospel, which creates a new family, one in which people are radically committed to one another's inclusion and well-being. This new family is to be marked by generosity, diversity, and love.

This raises a simple question: Are our communities more recognizable for these values, or for cultural values? Are we more easily recognized for what bonds us spiritually, or what bonds us as a demographic? What are the "laws" that form our communal identity among our churches today? What are the practices and behaviors that define it? What are the borders we defend? What is held in common almost universally among gathered believers in your church? And I'm not talking about *beliefs*, as important as those are; I'm talking about practices and a way of life that's held in common.

I had a friend who was a musician, who traveled around to many churches and played music. He said you could define each denomination by what store they bought their clothes in at a mall. This one went to Old Navy; that one went to J.Crew. This one went to Wal-Mart; that one went to Buckle. In one case, this kind of "branding" is literal and intentional. At a church I once visited, one of the musicians showed me the official dress code for volunteers (like greeters) and musicians. It required that they wear dark jeans (and suggested brands) and "cool, graphic T-shirts or shirts with the [CHURCH NAME REDACTED] logo."

Herein is plenty of fodder for both comedy and tragedy. But these instances make explicit what is implicit in almost any faith community. The church often gathers around values that have nothing to do with the gospel or with generosity, diversity, and love. Do these cultural "laws"—how you dress, shop, vote, and so on—define our churches more than our beliefs and spiritual practices do? Are we more easily defined as a marketing demographic or a community of faith?

The laws that defined Jewish identity in the Old Testament unified them and made them distinct from their neighbors. They were called to beliefs and practices that transcended class. In the church the distinction is in the character and beliefs of the church—in its transcultural uniting power. If we fail to live that out, then we are not the light of the world. We are instead assimilated. We are Mordecai.

THE TEMPTATIONS OF EXILE

When you find yourself living in exile, you are tempted in two directions: conformity and isolation. In conformity, assimilation works. You adopt the worldview, ethics, and way of life of the surrounding culture, and you experience deep change inside and out. In isolation, you hedge yourself into closed enclaves where the culture can't get in and your own culture can't get out. They are equally paths of ease. It's easy to conform, and you're richly rewarded for it. It's also easy to hedge in and protect yourself. But both lead to failures. Assimilation is a failure of nerve, and isolation is a failure of heart. Assimilation fails to resist; isolation fails to love.

Among the exiles in Babylon, both temptations reared their heads. Some wanted to hole up in ghettos, resist the pressures of Babylonian society, and wait for Yahweh to come and rescue them. Others thought, "When in Babylon, do as the Babylonians do." The prophet Jeremiah called for a third way:

> This is what the LORD Almighty, the God of Israel, says to all those I carried into exile from Jerusalem to Babylon: "Build houses and settle down; plant gardens and eat what they produce. Marry and have sons and daughters; find wives for your sons and give your daughters in marriage, so that they too may have sons and daughters. Increase in number there; do not decrease. Also, seek the peace and prosperity of the city to which I have carried you into exile. Pray to the LORD for it, because if it prospers, you too will prosper." (Jer. 29:4–7 NIV)[6]

The prophet was rejecting both assimilation and isolation, calling the people of God to maintain their identity as Jews while settling down and seeking the good of the city. Make a life in the city, God was saying, and work to make it a better place.

This is the path Daniel took. He served the Babylonian king, but only insofar as his well-formed conscience could allow. He wouldn't bow to their idols, he wouldn't eat their food, and he wouldn't obey their laws when they told him not to pray. But he served as a vizier to the king, and Babylon was a better place for his civic leadership. He demonstrated love toward his city and led it well, even while continuing his bold witness to another world and another way of life.

The same temptations the exiles faced exist for us today. In ways both overt and subtle, Christians are under pressure to conform to the values of a secular age. The overt ways are reported and debated regularly on cable news. The subtle ones are even more powerful.

You can see it in how ideas about sexuality get formed, as I described in the previous chapter. You can also see it in how the church itself takes on the features of mass culture: a focus on entertainment, the celebritization of pastors, an obsession with novelty, technology, and innovation that leaves tradition in the dust. These symptoms reveal a kind of permeability in both our souls and our institutions. We're being shaped and changed by the world around us, and in many cases (most?) we do so without giving it a second thought.

For the Babylonians, exile was the catalyst for immersion and assimilation. In our day, geographical exile isn't necessary. Immersion happens through mass culture—television, movies, music, social media, and ever-evolving mobile technology. These forces not only work on our imaginations through stories and ideas, they change the way we live our lives.

Consider how constant access to information and entertainment has reshaped the way we live. If you're old enough to have been an adult without a smartphone, you know what I mean. There was once a time when we weren't perpetually accessible and where entertainment and information weren't a tap away. A trip to the doctor's office or a ride in a taxi or an airplane ran the risk of being dull or cut you off from your community.

Today, you are accessible in so many ways: phone calls, text messages, emails, and instant messages from any number of social media platforms. Your life is on display as well, and that knowledge—that people are paying attention to what you do on Facebook, Twitter, and the rest—gives ordinary life a performative quality.

I see this in myself. Attending a concert or going to a restaurant isn't just a chance to see music or eat a great meal; it's a chance to tell people that I'm doing these things. And that is part of life in our particular version of Babylon. We feel as though we're on TV all the time. And all of this can easily be dismissed as silly or fun; yet, in reality, it's soul shaping.

We don't often think of technology this way. We don't imagine that it makes us who we are. But how *couldn't* it have profound effects? The average person, according to one study, checks his or her phone eighty-five times a day and spends about five hours a day using apps or browsing online.[7] That's nearly a third of our waking life. Our phones have become such a part of our life that we hardly notice them, and we hardly notice the constant ironies and hypocrisy that comes with them. I've seen several friends post photos of "cell phone stacks" on Instagram—the idea being that for a meeting or a meal, everyone stacks their phone upside down on top of each other so we're not distracted. The irony, of course, is that there's at least one phone missing from the photo: the one taking the picture and displaying the stack for others. A good idea (time detached from our phones for real, human connection) becomes a performance.

Our thoughtless participation in a consumeristic culture of perpetual entertainment is as clear a sign as any of our assimilation into our own secular Persia. We can sprinkle holy water on it by throwing Christian media consumerism into the mix (Christian media, books, conferences, etc.) and by enshrining Christian celebrities alongside the Miley Cyruses of the world, but, ultimately, most of us are deeply ingrained in a soul-forming way of life in service of consumption, distraction, and idolatry.

Sometimes we laugh at these ironies and contradictions, but such laughter is just a pretense. It's a way to wink and acknowledge that we're "in the know"[8] about irony, even as we indulge in the thing we're mocking.

"Hahaha, isn't it stupid how people take pictures of stuff like this?"

"Yeah . . . hold still. The image is getting blurry . . ."

"I mean, it's just ridiculous that you would take a photo and caption it, 'Not using my phone tonight!'"

"I know. People are gonna think it's hilarious when we get it posted."

When we participate in a culture with an eye-rolling, "I know, right?" attitude, we feel elevated above it, but that's just an illusion. At the end of the day, we're still seeking the dopamine hit that we get from likes, reposts, favorites, and so forth. We're still participating.

ASSIMILATED LIFE

There was a Jew named Mordecai living in Susa the citadel.

There was a Jew with a Persian name living at the center of power of a conquering empire.

There was one of God's people who'd lost or discarded his identity and embraced the way of life of a foreign world.

And there is each of us.

CHAPTER 3

THE GIRL WITH TWO NAMES

ACT THREE: ESTHER 2:7–18

The order went out throughout the kingdom, and the business of rounding up the beautiful virgins of Persia began. The king would bed each girl in turn, and one lucky winner would be his queen.

What would you do? Send your daughter to live with faraway relatives? Quickly marry her off? We'd like to think we'd resist . . . but we have no stories of resistance in Esther. Mostly, with somber order, soldiers and officials knocked on doors, watched daughters kiss their parents good-bye, and moved on. The girls—some terribly young—grouped together. Some whispered their fears. Some wept. They all marched to a palace that loomed over the city and would swallow them forever.

Mordecai had a cousin, a girl with two names. She lived with Mordecai because she was an orphan, and it seems likely that she had two names because her parents gave her one—Hadassah—and Mordecai gave her the other—Esther. She was like his daughter, and he knew the fate that awaited her as he sent her away. He did not resist and risk the lions or the furnace.

And so, this beautiful girl prepared to leave.

"Make friends with Hegai, the head of the harem. If he likes you, life will be much better for you. Do whatever he says. Follow his instructions to the letter. He knows what Xerxes likes, and he's a good ally to have if you are confined to the harem. Eat what he says. Follow the exercise and beauty regimen. Do your best to please him, and you'll be all the more likely to please the king."

It's a far cry from Daniel, who refused to eat at the king's table. Hegai in particular had one job: make sure the king was sexually satisfied. Mordecai sent Esther with the same mission.

The whole thing was sexist, exploitative, and misogynistic. But to be sure, Xerxes was an equal-opportunity exploiter. If you were a man, you'd be conscripted into the army and sent to fight in campaigns like the great failure in Greece, or sent to guard the boundaries from the horseback warriors in the north. In Persia, everyone was at the mercy of the king. At the same time, if Esther had been a man, she'd have had a shield. And the chance to raise a family.

"Be sure," Mordecai said, "you don't tell them you're a Jew."

The soldiers came to the gate. Mordecai blessed Esther and kissed her. She was gone.

I imagine that Mordecai was conflicted. There was Mordecai the Jew, who watched his cousin walk toward what was likely a life of imprisonment. And there was Mordecai the Persian—named for Marduk—who did his civic duty and who perhaps held a glimmer of hope that she would rise above the rest, transcend the harem, and wear the crown. Maybe he was callous, though. All we know for sure is that he willingly sent her away.

But Esther didn't enter the palace without resources. She was more than beautiful; she was smart, and she had Mordecai's sense for people and politics.

So, she was taken to the palace, placed in the harem, and would perhaps never be seen or heard from again.

Time passed. Mordecai heard very little. News came in bits and pieces. Esther had indeed befriended Hegai. He was taken with her beauty and her skill with people. She obeyed his every command. She learned to live a life that was solely meant to please the king. Diet, fitness, beautification routines. She was the most eager and disciplined student.

Young girls came and went. Those who didn't pass Hegai's exacting standards were sent away. One by one, the others were summoned by the king, only to return, sullen. Each knew the odds were stacked against her, but they could not help but hope to be the queen. Returning to the harem sealed their fate, one that was always and only sorrowful. They'd never marry. Never know love. Never have a real family, though they might birth children. They would be like prisoners, called upon only to serve the king's pleasure, and perhaps left in isolation for the rest of their lives.

Months passed. A year. And then word came. Esther was summoned by the king, and he was mesmerized by her.

Preparing to meet the king took on a contest-like quality, with each girl jockeying for the chance to become the queen. Some of them probably sang; some danced or told stories; others looked for more salacious ways to dazzle and entertain the king. But in Esther, the king encountered something different. She was beautiful, for sure, but she had a knack for winning the favor of everyone she met.

In one Jewish commentary, Esther is described as being like a sculpture where each beholder saw what they longed for in her face. She was like the Mirror of Erised in *Harry Potter*.

If that's true, then while the other girls came to him looking to delight his senses, Esther came to him with the power to provoke his greatest weakness. This was not Xerxes the Great, remember, but a defeated and humiliated king, and this beautiful girl, a girl with secrets, a girl who—as we'll see later—had political savvy and insight into the way people thought and worked . . . this girl came with a very different set of skills than any lyre player or singer or storyteller.

The king fell in love with the girl who preyed on his humanity.

Esther was named queen. Mordecai sighed in relief. She was still captive, but she was more than a mere slave.

The king ordered a feast. The city roared with life. Esther appeared before them, looking older, much more beautiful, more powerful than before. She wore the crown as if she were born to. Hegai stood nearby, beaming, his mission of pleasing the king accomplished. She was, after all, his handiwork, and her promotion was good for them both.

And Mordecai hoped it was good for him too.

CAPTIVITY

Captive is a deliberate word. There's a parallel between what happened to Esther and what had already happened to the Jews. In fact, the story of Esther is in harmony with a repetitive cycle in the Old Testament: Jews are assimilated, they are made captive, and they are called to repentance, to return to their identity as God's people. The great sin of the Old Testament is assimilation or capitulation to the world around them: foreign gods, foreign wives, unclean practices. Israel was to be set apart and distinct. When they lose their hard edges, when they lose touch with their distinctive way of life, calamity ensues.

And lose touch they did. Whether it was Baal worship, marriage to foreign women, construction of phallic Asherah poles, or defiling the temple with idol worship, Israel struggled in almost every generation to remain faithful. After years of prophetic warnings, the nation crumbled, and they were overtaken by the Babylonians.

Mordecai assimilated in Persia, and now Esther was taken captive by the Persian king. It was captivity within captivity.

Consider Esther's names, for instance. Names, in the Old Testament, almost always have some greater, symbolic meaning. Jacob was renamed "Israel" after he wrestled with God. Isaac means "laughter" because of the absurdity of his birth. Abram became Abraham. Simon, Peter. Saul, Paul.

Esther's two names reveal her split identity. She was Hadassah, a Hebrew, and Esther, a Persian, named after the Persian goddess

Ishtar (like Mordecai after Marduk). Names defined them, and Mordecai and Esther were clearly defined by their Persian identities. Esther spoke the Persian language; she could pass for a Persian. Other than Mordecai, no one knew she wasn't Persian. For Jews, these were red flags and deep sins.

But she was not entirely disconnected from her roots. She had a Hebrew name, Hadassah, which comes from the Hebrew word for "myrtle." The name Myrtle, some of the Jewish commentaries say,[1] was meant to imply "righteous," as in Zechariah 1:8, where the prophet envisioned a man on a red horse standing among myrtle trees. The myrtles were said to represent righteous ones, and Esther stood like a righteous one (by virtue of her Jewish identity) among the Persians. Righteousness, in this sense, was simply by the nature of her Jewish identity. She was righteous because she was not actually one of them.

She was also, by most accounts, quite beautiful. And myrtles smell good. So there's that.

And still we're not done with her name yet. Just as Ahasuerus is a pun on "headache," Esther is a pun on the Hebrew word for "hidden." Hiddenness is a theme that follows her throughout the book. She passed for a Persian, and for most of the book, no one knew she was Jewish.

And as I've already noted, God, too, is hidden in the story, in part because no one seemed to seek him. His name isn't mentioned once in the whole book of Esther. This whole story seemingly happened without his direct intervention, and yet, what unfolds in the story can't be seen as anything less than a miracle. God was at work, but he was hidden. This should comfort us, as we will see.

THE TROUBLE WITH ESTHER (AND OTHER BIBLE HEROES)

We need to be careful how far we go with hiddenness. Sometimes Esther's hiddenness gets exaggerated; in some readings of her story, she hid her identity not because she was assimilated, but because she was kind of a spy. In one account from the Talmud, Esther was secretly married to Mordecai, was only unfaithful to him once, when she had to be, and would sneak away to see him whenever she could.

This is an example of a common problem for Bible readers. People want their Bible characters to be the good guys. We like thinking of Jacob and Noah as heroes, while we ignore that one was a swindler and the other was a drunk. We think of Joseph and his Technicolor Dreamcoat, ignoring how easily he assimilated in Egypt and the cruel shame he heaped on his brothers. We also forget that Joseph was the first Jewish slave in Egypt, and when he moved his family into Egypt with him, it resulted in four hundred years of slavery. Bible characters are complex, and their legacies—even the best of them—are decidedly mixed. Esther *was* a victim of a despot. But she proved herself excellent at living the Persian life and preparing for the king's bed.

But why did Mordecai let her be taken in the first place?

Where was his Liam Neeson moment, where he confronts the kidnappers and promises to unleash holy vengeance if they don't bring her back? Why not resist? Why not escape? It's easy to understand Esther's role here; she was subject to the will of her king *and* her cousin. And the language of the text is very passive in this respect. She was *taken*.

But that doesn't excuse it either. Mordecai was not giving Esther to marry the king—bad enough in itself—he was letting her be taken as a concubine.

We have to ask a couple of questions here: Did Mordecai not take his religion seriously? Was he unconcerned with the consequences of letting his cousin be defiled by a foreign king? Or was he simply unconcerned with her fate? Was he like David Puddy on *Seinfeld*, who told Elaine he wasn't concerned about her lack of religious beliefs because "I'm not the one going to hell." After all, Mordecai didn't have to face the lust of the king or a life behind the doors of the harem. Esther was a sacrifice, sent to suffer a terrible fate for the sake of her cousin.

While the language around her captivity is passive, once she was inside, she was anything but. She dived in, taking on the fitness and beauty regimen with vigor, impressing the head of the harem and ultimately the king himself.

This, too, was a compromise. Esther can't be painted as merely a victim. She isn't a martyr. She had an alliance of sorts with Hegai, the head eunuch, whose sole job was to satisfy the king's sexual appetites with the supply of the harem. When the king was looking for a queen among them, Hegai's job was to provide one, and Esther—smart, beautiful, and eager to learn—made a great candidate.

One of the rabbinical commentaries describes Esther as a work of art in which every beholder can see what they want.[2] Her skill was to "find favor in the eyes of all that looked upon her" (2:15, author's translation). It was this skill, far more than anything sexual, that won her favor with the king.

The text is a black box when it comes to her motives, of course. We only see the actions, which leave a lot of questions unanswered. But the circumstances show how muddled her situation was, which is why I think her story is so important for us.

LIVING A COMPROMISED LIFE

Just as we're tempted to flatten Esther, Mordecai, Jacob, and Joseph into two-dimensional stories of heroes, we want to tell simple stories about ourselves, and it's easier to grasp that we're either sinners or saints than it is to acknowledge that we're a mix of both.

The truth is, our own motivations are just as much a black box as Esther's. We're a mystery to ourselves, and if we saw our lives from the outside—much as we might see the lives of our friends or spouses if we really looked closely—we'd find a similar mix. Why do we do the things we do? Why are we entangled in some cultural practices we don't like, whether it's mindless consumption, lustful indulgence, or idolizing politicians and celebrities? Why do we find some moments in our lives easy to be a person of faith, and others so hard?

There may be some uncompromised Christians out there, managing to walk that tightrope between assimilation and isolation, but I suspect most of us teeter on one side or the other, and unless you're living in a compound in Idaho, it's likely the assimilation side.

The gravity that draws us there is incredibly powerful. For Mordecai, the gravity was life in the citadel, life at the seat of power and influence. Esther's own gravity might have been a number of things. Self-preservation, certainly, but power, glamour, influence. Let's not pretend those temptations and emotions weren't as real and present to her as they might be to us.

What's remarkable about the story isn't so much what's present (in terms of motives) as what's absent. Faith in God and identity as a Jew didn't seem to enter into the equation except that Mordecai urged Esther to keep it hidden.

And as I've already said, God is hidden too. Mordecai and Esther's story appears to be caught up purely in the world of human affairs, a world of power and politics and lust.

THE POWER OF MYTHOLOGY

Behind both Esther's and Mordecai's stories lies a grand backdrop of mythology. And it is that myth—more than simple human weakness, more than fear, more than failure of heart or nerve—that makes sense of all that we see in the story of Esther.

Xerxes was a god in a pantheon of gods, and his loss at war faded his glory but didn't extinguish it. Everything about Persian society still pointed to his immortality, his power, and his total dominance of their world. There was even a divine way of talking about his loss to the Greeks—it was the triumph not only of Greek hoplites and superior tactics, but of the Greek gods over the Persian gods.

To reckon with Xerxes was to reckon with immense, entrenched, mythologized power, and to live in his world was to be perpetually reminded of and bombarded by it. In the comfort of our own modern understanding of the world, we can see Xerxes as a mere human being, but it was nearly impossible to do so from where Mordecai and Esther sat. In part, that impossibility was enforced by Xerxes' own expressions of power.

The myth of Xerxes' divinity was made manifest in the grandiosity, wealth, and power of his empire. It was hard not to get swept up into belief.

So Mordecai handed over Esther, and Esther complied. The myths of Persia had captured them. They had a hard time seeing the world in any other way. The all-powerful king—referred to as the "King of Kings"—had demanded her, and the myth supposed that she belonged to him, one way or another, anyway. There are layers of lies here: the absolute will of the king versus the will of the girl, the ownership of the king's subjects, the absence of any exercise of will over one's own sexuality. These dehumanizing, dignity-destroying ideas were entrenched in the culture of Persia, and they became entrenched in Persia's citizens.

Here again we need to be wary of creating too great a sense of distance between their world and ours. We'd like to think we live in a world where mythologies have been put away for good, but we would be wrong. Instead, we've simply exchanged our myths, exchanged the ways we enthrone power, and exchanged the ways that power expresses itself.

THE POWER OF WOUNDS

We, too, are enslaved and abused by our culture. Think of all the ways our world tells us we're inadequate, and all the ways it tries to sell us on something else that will ultimately make us happy. We can laugh at the absurdity of it all, but given how relentless it is, we should also weep. Our whole consumer economy is designed to prey on our sense of weakness and our longings, and it works. We are an anxious, rootless, desperate world.

Life has enough trauma and pain on its own. The world around us is a deeply sad place. We routinely see disease drain the life out of friends and loved ones. One in thirty-six college-aged women report being raped, and 88 percent of women who graduate from college report some degree of physical or sexual abuse.[3] Any nightly news report reveals a world full of war, conflict, and natural disasters.

And there are the smaller traumas, which nonetheless leave

their scars. There are haunting childhood experiences of shame and loneliness. There are the wounds left from broken homes. There are lost and broken friendships, tales of betrayal and abandonment.

There are also vicarious traumas. We are ourselves trapped while watching the suffering of others. In my life, I've watched a loved one suffer the consequences of harassment from a sexual predator. I've seen how deep those wounds are, how horrific the feeling of powerlessness is, the way it left her feeling anxious and unsafe at the slightest trigger for more than a decade. I've seen chronic illness leave my wife unable to eat or sleep or walk around the house. She wakes some mornings feeling as if she has broken glass in her joints, or she crashes late in the day when her energy level inexplicably collapses. I've seen her deal with a thousand insensitive comments, ranging from suggestions that she change her diet, her medicine, or her doctor to recommendations of certain oils and vitamins and workout routines. Each person is subtly claiming that he or she has the key to resolving my wife's problems, blissfully unaware of the myriad ways we've already fought the disease. Hers is the deeper pain, but I carry it with her. I sit, powerless, as it unfolds, and I know that I'll never be capable of healing her, and its impact scars me too.

We all have similar stories. Our wounds send us searching for solutions or for meaning. We pour ourselves into work, thinking success might heal us, or into our social lives, thinking esteem and affirmation from others might be enough. We numb ourselves with food, drink, entertainment, and sex.

In a secular age, when we're unhindered by any larger sense of morality, we go looking in the previously forbidden corners, trying to salve our wounds. A *New York Times Magazine* article from May 2017 told the story of several couples exploring open marriages in hopes of saving their marriages.[4] The article *strained* to put a positive spin on it, and the author even questioned her own commitment to monogamy, but in all, the stories were tragic. Several marriages profiled ended in divorce. They were full of jealousy and secrets. Numerous people went along with the decision to open the marriage in the twisted hope of saving the marriage. One couple asked the third party to move in with them, like *Three's Company*, but with no reason to laugh.

The story radiated with deep sadness. These deeply wounded people—like you, like me—were searching for happiness in the most tragic of places. Hidden in the story of the main couple being profiled, in a comment that was almost a throwaway detail, they mentioned that during their journey toward open marriage, they "continued on, volunteering at church." Now, I know there are all kinds of churches, and certainly there are some that have become degraded enough to smile on polyamory, but nonetheless, it's a point worth noting. It's hard for me to imagine a more stunning example of assimilation.

It's easy to sit in the seat of judgment on these things, and there's a place for calling out evil for what it is. We don't love our neighbors well if we fail to speak up when we see them inflicting harm on themselves.

But we also don't love them well if we fail to see the wounds that send them—like us—looking for answers in the wrong places. Humanity is both responsible for its fallenness and cursed by it. Both sinner and saint. A fallen world and a host of evil spiritual forces are wreaking havoc on our souls, and the tantalizing power of idols lies in their offer to heal our wounds.

Why did Esther and Mordecai cooperate with the king's decree? Why did Esther conform to life in the harem, preparing for her night with the king? Why did Mordecai assimilate as a Persian and work to find a place at the center of power in the realm?

One answer could be that they were calloused and craven, eager to abandon their identity as Jews. Another that they were citizens of a craven world, far from home, and daily suffering the traumas imposed by the pluralistic and oppressive world around them. Maybe their wounds drove them to seek power and status as much as their sinful hearts did. Maybe they thought that power, sex, and glamour would make them feel whole.

Maybe Esther's two names are not only a symbol of compromise but a symbol of woundedness and loss—the loss of her parents, the loss of her homeland, the loss of a way of life as one of God's people.

If so, it makes all that's to come an even deeper story of God's grace. Not only can he use the lives of people hardened by rebellion, he can also use those who are crushed by it, whose souls and consciences are tattered and seared. In this way, we see Esther as someone who is three-dimensional: compromised and assimilated and in need of repentance, but also traumatized and broken and in need of healing.

And maybe that description is shorthand for life in a fallen world. What follows, then, should inspire hope for us all.

CHAPTER 4

RESISTANCE

ACT FOUR: ESTHER 2:13-3:5

It was late. The sun was mostly hidden now behind the western edge of Susa, and the markets were closed. The feast of Esther had come to an end, and the city had returned to normal routines. Fires in courtyards. Thin, feral dogs darting between the alleys. And on that night in particular, Mordecai, making his way to the king's gate.

It wasn't merely a gate, but a grand entry hall to the palace, where the politically minded jockeyed for position and influence, shouting about taxes and tariffs and listening for rumors from within the palace. Mordecai spent most of his days there. He was a regular part of the city's political scene.

That night was different. Mordecai approached with a sense of urgency. The courtyard at the king's gate was empty except for the guards, who looked mostly bored. Mordecai entered the courtyard and leaned, arms crossed, against a wall near the entrance to the palace. The guards eyed him and turned away, disinterested. A shadow emerged from the palace doors, tall and thin, one of the eunuchs from Esther's entourage. He said something to the guard and turned to Mordecai, waving him over. The guards ignored him as he passed, following the eunuch into the palace.

Through the door, into another courtyard with stone pavers. More guards there, just as disinterested as they entered another building. It was dark and smelled like stones from a river, like moss and mold and earth.

They passed through a long corridor with narrow windows, into the courtyard. The eunuch was silent and quick, and Mordecai kept the pace.

Soon they came to a dead end with a large wooden door on iron hinges. The eunuch strained to pull it open, and Mordecai followed him inside. Together they pulled it shut.

Inside was a large room. A hearth with no fire sat at the far end. There were low tables and cushions in the center; it was a feasting hall. Dead torches sat at regular intervals.

A mural, inscrutable in the shadows, filled the nearby wall. A single lamp burned at the opposite end of the room, held by a tall figure standing in a doorway that mirrored their own. When Mordecai and the eunuch stepped into the room, the tall figure turned to the corridor behind him, saying something into the darkness. Moments later, two girls appeared, one in large, heavy robes, with a cloak over her head. The other—an attendant, Mordecai guessed—close at her side.

Mordecai walked toward her, the eunuch close at his side. The other eunuch stepped in front of the girls, meeting Mordecai in the middle of the room.

"Mordecai," said Esther, removing her hood. She turned to the eunuchs. "Leave us," she ordered. She turned to the attendant. "You too. Stand by the door. This won't be long."

They stepped away, leaving Mordecai and Esther in the center of the dark room alone.

Mordecai bowed low, greeting Esther not as his cousin, but as his queen. She nodded her head low, too, honoring the cousin who had raised her as would a father.

In the low light, he could see a crown nestled in the braids of her hair, the silver threads crisscrossing her tunic. He smelled the spices and oils on her glowing skin. She was the product of a life of luxury. But when she smiled, he saw Hadassah.

"You aren't safe," he said. "It's why I insisted on coming to see you."

"What do you mean?" she asked.

"I was at the king's gate. There were rumors today—bloody ones. There is money to be made when a fight breaks out, especially if that fight means civil war, so the traders are all licking their chops. Some would like to see your king dead."

Esther shook her head dismissively. "Many would like to see him dead. Do you see where we are? How safe this palace is?"

"But what if the threat is from inside the palace?"

Esther said nothing.

"Their names are Bigthan and Teresh," he whispered. Eunuchs who served as part of the king's entourage. "They're embittered, and they've been plotting."

"You know this how?"

"I know this because I'm a man who knows things."

Esther nodded. "What do I do?"

"Send word to the king. It won't be hard to prove this true. They're fools, and everyone is talking about their plans."

"So everyone knows but Xerxes?"

"Everyone knows but Xerxes." Mordecai nodded. "He doesn't seem quick to notice his surroundings."

He paused, taking in her face again. "Have they learned that you're a Jew?"

"No. Just as you said, I kept it to myself."

"Good," Mordecai said. "It's safer for you that way."

"As you've said."

He took her face in his hands, whispered a blessing in Hebrew, kissed her forehead, and left.

Two days later, Mordecai arrived at the king's gate to see the twisted bodies of Bigthan and Teresh impaled on stakes, like birds pierced with arrows, frozen in time and space.

The king brooded. He paced. Advisors stood near the door as he walked a circuit from the table to the window to the fire, again and again. He sweated. He swore. He wiped his brow on the sleeve of his robe. He breathed in staggering gasps. Suddenly he heaved an empty pot at a wall, then a pitcher filled with wine. They erupted and shattered. The advisors tried to make themselves small, shrinking into the walls, eyeing their surroundings for cover.

Xerxes paused, breathed heavily, found his own cup and lifted it, only to find it empty. He looked back at the bleeding corpse of the pitcher as the wine spread between the stone pavers on the floor. He turned to the advisors.

"Who else?"

Silence.

"Who else?" Louder this time. A bead of sweat formed on his temple and began to crawl down the side of his face. "Who else?" His voice made them shrink again.

"We don't know," ventured one of them. "We think it may just have been the two."

"It makes no sense. What would they possibly gain?"

"Maybe they . . . just had a grudge," said one.

Another: "Maybe they didn't like being eunuchs."

Nervous laughs. The king grinned. Then he sent his empty cup sailing over their heads. It clattered against the wall and bounced off a fat advisor's head. He dropped to his knees, more in fear than pain, and slowly made his way back to standing, rubbing his head. He raised his eyes to see the king glaring at him. He dropped his hand.

"It's clear to me that things have changed in Susa," said another voice. "Not to mention Persia itself." It was Haman, standing apart, lean, dressed more like a soldier than a counselor to the king, his hair long and grey. He leaned against a column, icy, watching the king's tantrum with disinterest, calculating his opening.

"How do you mean?" asked the king.

"You've conquered, you've made peace, you've given the kingdom feast after feast, but there remains an . . . unsteadiness. You have a kingdom to rule, but you have a city of conspirators. And"—he raised his eyes, looked to the king, the advisors, and the king again—"an ineffective council."

One of the advisors stood tall and took a step forward. "Now, just one second—"

"They're silent until you tell them they're worthless," Haman said.

"You've needed us for trade, for governance, for solving disputes."

"And you've failed him on security."

Silence. The king looked at each of them.

"You need a vizier," said Haman. "No more of this clamor of voices. Someone with your strength and authority, looking where you cannot look, ruling in your name where you cannot be, rooting out the liars and conspirators and extortioners from your midst. No more of this haggling with the people at the king's gate. Show them your strength. If they can't live in peace while you shower them with food and festivals, then they'll live in peace when you make them fear you. Remind them that you're not just their ruler; you're their god."

"Sir," started one advisor.

"Be still," said the king. He eyed Haman. "And you'd be that vizier? You'd be like my eyes and ears?"

"Your very presence. And your fist."

Xerxes turned to the window. Susa spread beneath him like patchwork. The courtyard at the king's gate was full of merchants, politicians, emissaries from distant branches of the empire. Their chatter rose like smoke. In the city itself, the markets swarmed with people. Awnings stretched over the flat rooftops. A flock of goats staggered through the streets to the west, to market, or to a butcher.

Xerxes himself held it all together. He kept the horse-back armies off in the distance, crushing anyone who would lay siege to the city. He kept the trade routes open, making men rich. And still, there were knives in the city aimed at his throat.

He looked back to the king's gate. The bodies of Bigthan and Teresh hung over the courtyard on their stakes, twisting by the hour as their drained bodies stiffened. The first of the birds had begun to settle on them.

He turned back to Haman. "My presence and my fist. So be it. I want these conspiracies uprooted. If blood needs to be shed, you'll shed it." To the advisors, "Haman's to be treated just as I would be. Take him to the king's gate. They need to know. You need to know. Do what he says."

The advisors looked at one another awkwardly. Haman stood expressionless. The one rubbing his head slowly dropped to one knee, then the other. He bowed his head.

Xerxes looked at the others. "Bow to him as you would to me. Then get out of my sight."

Word of a big announcement spread through the city, and Mordecai made his way back to the king's gate. The crowd was thick. It poured out beyond the courtyard, onto the steps and streets beyond. From a distance, on the platform near the entrance to the palace, he could make out several figures. The crowd was hushed, but the voices didn't carry.

Mordecai began to make his way through the crowd. Some, knowing who he was, allowed him to pass. Others forced him to press through. He heard Bigthan's and Teresh's names. He saw Haman on the platform, heard his name spoken, heard the word *vizier*, an audible gasp from the crowd, and saw the advisors near Haman drop to their knees as Haman stepped forward. The kneeling moved like a wave from the platform through the crowd, each row bowing, one after another. It passed Mordecai and spread beyond him.

"Mordecai," a nearby voice said, "they've ordered this. He's the new vizier to the king. We're to treat him as we would Xerxes."

Mordecai didn't move. Didn't blink. He stared at Haman, who smiled pompously over the crowd.

"Mordecai," said another voice.

"I won't bow to him," Mordecai answered.

"Mordecai . . ." one man pleaded.

Haman spotted Mordecai. His eyes narrowed.

"I won't bow to Haman," he repeated.

"What's wrong with you? Are you a fool?"

"No. But I am a Jew. And I will not bow."

This exact phrase passed through the crowd and found its way to Haman's own ears. And that's how the crisis began.

THE TWO MORDECAIS

Strange things were happening here. One moment, Mordecai was being a good Persian and protecting the life of the king. The next, he was refusing to obey the king's command. It seems he should either have supported the coup or should have bowed, but not both. At least then he would be consistent.

But these two decisions had very different motivations. While they appear inconsistent, they actually reveal the character of Mordecai, and they highlight the tension of the book.

In the first place, we have a very pragmatic and political decision. Mordecai, who "was sitting at the king's gate," as the Scriptures put it (2:21), was trying to have a culture-shaping political influence in Persia. He was a politician to the degree that one can be a politician in a dictatorship, particularly a dictatorship where the king is revered as a god.

The king's gate—which archaeologists refer to as the "Gate of All Nations"[1]—is where everyone coming and going from the palace would pass. If you wanted an audience with the king, you'd pass this way. Mordecai hung out here to get the latest political gossip and, presumably, to try to have some influence on those affairs. He was an assimilated Jew; he looked like a Persian, he lived like a Persian, and he blended in.

His intervention in the plot against the king, then, was consistent with this picture of Mordecai. This was Mordecai the politician, Mordecai who had raised his cousin to pass for a Persian, who'd prepared her to make the innumerable compromises necessary to thrive in the harem, win the king, and become the queen of Persia without anyone suspecting she was a Jew.

But that's not all.

To protect the king is also consistent with God's word to the exiles in Jeremiah 29—to work for the peace of the city. The death of the emperor wasn't likely to bring about a greater peace. More likely, it would result in some kind of power struggle among the aristocracy, send the palace reeling, and possibly bring about war. Persia was a massive empire, with Xerxes as its great figurehead—the god who conquered everyone and who held them all together. If he died, then it's very possible (and maybe likely) that some of the far-flung peoples of the empire might have thought it was a good time to stop paying homage and tribute to the empire, and this would mean war.

Lastly, we can also understand Mordecai's actions as fatherly. He went directly to Esther, as if to warn her in particular of the impending danger. It not only earned Mordecai points with the king, but it further cemented Esther's position in the palace when she revealed the plot.

Haman's appointment was a response to the plot, and it was a consolidation of power into the hands of one man. The king, fearful of more plots, wanted to crack down on the city, and so put his faith in one man to bring order. Haman relished the power and demanded the same subservience from the court as did the king. Thus, the bowing.

But Mordecai wouldn't bow. It was a crucial moment in his life, and a moment that required tremendous courage.

Haman was now the embodiment of the idolatry of power. He was vested with all the king's authority, and in a world where authority was likened to divinity, the symbolism of bowing was much more than a sign of deference. It was a recognition of this divinity-authority connection, and it was an act of worship. Mordecai's conscience was pushed to its limits, and now—like Daniel before him, who would not worship Darius—Mordecai wouldn't bow.

It was a moment of spiritual awakening, forced in part by the fact that Haman was an Agagite.

AN ANCIENT CONFLICT

We need to zoom out for a moment to make sense of this. The story is marching toward an attempted genocide of the Jewish people, driven by this Agagite. Agag was the king of the Amalekites, defeated by Saul in 1 Samuel 15, and though God's instructions were to wipe out the Amalekites completely, it seems that at least one line of descendants remained. Calling Haman an Agagite ties him to Agag, the Amalekites, and a war against the Jews that goes all the way back to the exodus, when they were the first to attack Israel in the desert.

Moses, in the book of Deuteronomy, warned Israel not to forget the horrors the Amalekites had inflicted on them:

"Remember what Amalek did to you on the way as you came out of Egypt, how he attacked you on the way when you were faint and weary, and cut off your tail, those who were lagging behind you, and he did not fear God. Therefore when the LORD your God has given you rest from all your enemies around you, in the land that the LORD your God is giving you for an inheritance to possess, you shall blot out the memory of Amalek from under heaven; you shall not forget." (25:17–19)

In Jewish tradition, the book of Esther is read every year at a festival called Purim (much more on this later). In many traditions within Judaism, this passage from Deuteronomy is read before Esther. It explains Haman's animosity toward Mordecai in particular and Jews in general. An Amalekite, Haman is in this reading predisposed not only to hatred but to murder. And more than murder, indiscriminate murder, even genocide.

Israel first faced the Amalekites shortly after receiving the law at Mount Sinai. The Amalekites attacked Israel from the rear, killing the stragglers, the weak, the sick, women and children. They were terrorists, seeking to demoralize the Jews long before engaging in direct conflict. One doesn't have to think hard to find parallels today, in those who target innocents in order to demoralize their enemies. It's a win-at-all-costs approach to power. There is no distinction made between the well-armed soldier and the sick child, between combatants and noncombatants. There are only ends, and means don't matter.

Israeli scholar Yoram Hazony wrote, "We have no idea what gods ruled over the Amalekites. None are named, and for all we know, there may have been none at all. What we do know is that whatever gods may have belonged to Amalek, as a people they did not fear any moral boundaries established by them. Unlike even the most depraved of the idolaters of Canaan, they respected no limits on their desire to control all as they found fit."[2]

People of faith get blamed for a lot of evil in a post-9/11 world. Religious terrorists killed thousands of Americans on that day, and in the years since, they've wreaked havoc the world over: terror attacks, ISIS, and more. At the same time, evangelical Christians have been increasingly seen as bullies and bigots, archaic jerks who don't want to bake cakes for their gay neighbors. The argument has been made more than once that religion itself is the problem, particularly when religion speaks of moral absolutes and eternal consequences. But the Amalekites offer a bold and terrifying counterexample—a community where, precisely because it was not religious, everything was possible, including the extermination of an entire people for the sake of the accumulation of power.

AN ANCIENT IDOL

Mordecai's refusal to bow wasn't just a rejection of Haman, and it wasn't just a symbol for the generations-long conflict between Israel and Amalek. It was a rejection of the idol of power. It may have been the moment of life change for Mordecai as well, a moment where all of his work in jockeying for position and influence—all those temptations that had led him to assimilate in Persia—no longer held sway for him. Suddenly, Mordecai realized he lived in a world that was bigger than the court, bigger than Susa, bigger than Persia itself. He was abruptly caught up in the story of God and Israel, and in that world, he could not bow. "Because I am a Jew," he said.

It was an act of courage and vulnerability, and it has echoes throughout the story of the Bible. Abraham left an aristocratic life in Ur to follow God into the wilderness. Moses sacrificed his position and power in Egypt to defend a slave being beaten, shedding blood in the process. Eventually he returned and made himself even more vulnerable, asking for Israel to be freed. David faced Goliath not in strength, but weakness. John the Baptist spoke truth to power, both in the religious establishment and the government. And then, of course, there is the incarnation itself, the ultimate act of vulnerability, the ultimate moment when someone laid down his power and authority for the sake of others.

In contrast, we have what we might call the spirit of Amalek. It's an approach to power that seeks to win at all costs, a willingness to commit great acts of evil to accomplish its own ends.

Living this way accumulates "collateral damage," which in war means the death of innocents. In business, it means burned-out employees and coworkers, embittered ex-clients, and broken laws. In our homes, it's lonely spouses and children, families starved for love and attention, an ecosystem that learns to tiptoe around someone's wrath.

Haman's rise marked an awakening in Mordecai as he

recognized the installation of a terrible power in Persia, one that threatened not only the Jews, but the realm itself.

RESISTANCE AND THE GOOD OF THE CITY

Mordecai's reaction was not solely about his own conscience. As noted earlier, his intervention that protected the king can easily be viewed as in accord with the call in Jeremiah 29 to work for the peace of the city. And here, too, in this act of civil disobedience, he can be seen to be working for the city's good.

A culture that idolizes power is going to become brutal. Power will become the solution to everything, and every challenge will be met with some expression of it. As much as the Persian Empire was already a powerful, brutal regime, it could be worse. And in the hands of Haman, it became much worse.

Haman's appointment marks a departure from the way Xerxes had—up to that point—been running things. Yoram Hazony has pointed out the difference between Esther 1–2 and Esther 3–7, which marks the reign of Haman as vizier.[3] In the earlier chapters (as well as after chapter 7), Xerxes was surrounded by a council. We hear the names of other advisors, and they guided him, for instance, to banish Vashti and issue the decree about husbands and wives. After the attempt on his life, the king cast them out, and authority was consolidated into the hands of one man. Mordecai's resistance, then, wasn't just spiritual; it was political. It was a refusal to endorse a new policy that concentrated power in the hands of a power-worshiping Amalekite and threatened the "peace of the city."

As compromised as he was, Mordecai had been pressed to a place where he could compromise no more. He awakened to his identity as a Jew and embraced it publicly as part of a protest against the idolization of power. "Here," he said, "I can go no further."

POWER, VULNERABILITY, AND VICTIMHOOD

There's a profound message here about the dangers and limits of power. As we'll see, Haman's own grasp for power was toxic—not only for the empire, but for himself. Mordecai had the foresight to resist that temptation, and he modeled a path of resistance that Esther, too, would follow. He embraced weakness. He embraced vulnerability.

Vulnerability is a buzzword right now. The writing and teaching of Brené Brown is incredibly popular, and her work focuses on shame, vulnerability, and what she calls "whole-hearted living."[4] In Christian circles, similar work (some inspired by Brown) has been offered by Chuck DeGroat, Curt Thompson, and Andy Crouch.

Vulnerability, as Crouch defines it, is a capacity for meaningful risk. That might mean risks taken on behalf of oneself, or risk on behalf of others. It has a thousand applications, and Crouch's work *Strong and Weak* explores both the personal and the social power of vulnerability.

But we have to be careful when we start talking about vulnerability, because in our culture today, there's something at work that *looks* like vulnerability but is actually a means of acquiring power. This is victimhood, and it's directly related to the values of a secular age.

If, as a culture, we've lost any rooted sense of morals or values, we also lose ways to navigate conflict and tension. We don't have language for it anymore because one person's definition of *good* is radically different from—and perhaps opposed to—someone else's. Even so, generally speaking, no one likes a bully, and it's still universally agreed that oppression is a bad thing. That fact provides leverage for cultural power; if you can claim victim status, and if you can point out the nearby bully who's oppressing you, you gain a tremendous amount of cultural power.[5]

The late philosopher René Girard described our culture as one obsessed with victims and scapegoats. Once you gain the status of victim, you rise above any kind of moral responsibility or scrutiny. The moral imperative is about justice: How do we defend these victims from their oppressors? Any sins of the victim can and will be overlooked because, after all, they only committed them in response to their oppressors. Victimhood can also empower others who would advocate on behalf of the victim. Girard wrote, "The victims most interesting to us are always those who allow us to condemn our neighbors. And our neighbors do the same. They always think first about the victims for whom they hold us responsible."[6]

Theologian Derek Rishmawy, writing about Girard, connects this to the cultural battlefield:

> Haven't you been agitated by that progressive who is always taking every chance they get to share a devastating story about some victim and immediately tacking the moral on that "this is what Republicans/Evangelicals/Fundamentalists views lead to" or some such statement? Or on the flipside, the way that some legal absurdity just shows the moral bankruptcy of the progressive/Democrat/Post-Evangelical capitulation? Doesn't this latest tragedy (beautifully) highlight their horrid lack of concern? (A concern which, quite admirably, *you* have). Don't these tear-stained faces cry out for the merciless prosecution of our enemies? (Oh, and yes, maybe some aid as well, of course.)[7]

Rishmawy shows the *power* of victimhood. By claiming the status of victim, you don't make yourself vulnerable to risk; you're actually insulating yourself from it. You shift the conversation to the oppressor. If there's a victim, who then is the victimizer, and how can we stop them and punish them for their deeds? You also justify all manner of behavior, because, after all, you're a victim; who can blame you for your overreactions or missteps?

This dynamic creates a race to the bottom of the cultural food chain. Everyone wants to see themselves as the oppressed ones because in doing so, they will find the necessary cultural leverage to gain power. So cultural progressives, activists, and the LGBT community point to conservatives and Christians who hold to orthodox convictions about sexuality and say, "Look at what you've done! Your insensitivity, your oppressive sexuality, your archaic ideas!" Likewise, conservatives and Christians look back at them and cry foul over religious liberty, freedom of speech, and more. Both sound like Dennis from *Monty Python and the Holy Grail*, shouting, "Help! Help! I'm being repressed!"

Even among Christians, there's been a great deal of this kind of behavior. On the one hand, there's someone like Jen Hatmaker, whose affirming stance on same-sex relationships has led to having her book pulled from the shelves of some retailers and speaking invitations revoked. On the other hand, we have people like Tim Keller, who was awarded and subsequently denied a prestigious Kuyper Prize from Princeton Seminary, largely for his beliefs about sexuality and gender.

In both cases the temptation—not just for Hatmaker and Keller, but also for their supporters—is to shout, "Victim!" But the question to ask is this: Are they truly the victims of mean-spirited oppressors? The answer *may indeed be yes*, but it isn't fair to paint *all* of their critics that way, and it likely isn't fair to paint *most* of their critics that way. Instead, we should ask if they're facing the consequences of oppression or the consequences of their own ideas.

I think the latter is often the case, and I think it's also the case that we don't like facing the consequences of our ideas. Just the other day, I saw an eruption on Twitter when a friend posted something provocative. People were (shockingly) provoked by it, and it led to one of those pages-long threads of replies and arguments. What was interesting was how quickly the conversation moved *away* from the original, provocative statement and into a weird argument about whether someone had the freedom to make such statements. It's an argument that I've seen often on Twitter; folks get angry not because of the substance of disagreement, and not because of the tone of disagreement, but because of the presence of disagreement at all. There's a sense that one's "freedom of expression" is dependent on freedom from dissent, which of course is ludicrous.

But the engine that drives these conversations isn't the logic of debate; it's the logic of victimhood. When confronted with disagreement or argument, one can shout, "Help! I'm being repressed!" and almost certainly find that the argument changes (dealing with the social dynamics rather than the substance of ideas) and help arrives. Because nobody likes a bully.

But ideas have consequences. And the difference between "playing the victim" and embracing vulnerability lies in the willingness to face those consequences.

EMBRACING REAL RISK

As Andy Crouch describes it, "The vulnerability that leads to flourishing requires risk, which is the possibility of loss—the chance that when we act, we will lose something we value."[8]

Victimhood isn't risky. Rather, it's a way of shaping a

cultural narrative. If we can define ourselves as victims, we can leverage the past to demonize our opponents in the present and accomplish our goals. Vulnerability, on the other hand, is about putting ourselves in harm's way. At its best, it means putting ourselves in harm's way for the sake of others.

Mordecai and Esther highlight the difference between vulnerability and victimhood. In each case, they deliberately took steps to put themselves in harm's way. Mordecai passed for a Persian. He had nothing to gain from revealing his Jewishness and refusing to bow; he only had something to lose. And yet, for the sake of his soul, for the sake of God's people, and for the good of the city, he refused to bow to Haman.

This is our invitation in a world gone mad. Rather than continue the race to the bottom of victimhood, we should look at our world, ask ourselves how faithfulness to our calling as God's people invites us to participate in it, and embrace the risks that might come with it.

At times, that will look like Mordecai's resistance, when we refuse to participate in something broadly accepted in our culture. Doing so will invite the wrath of those around us, but vulnerability calls us to do it anyway.

At other times, it may be that we're called to take action—to start a business or a charity, to look for needs in our cities, our schools, and our neighborhoods—in hopes of making the city a more peaceful and flourishing place. Surely, as the march of culture continues toward madness, doing this will invite risks too. People might discover that you're a Christian and call into question your every step, your every action. Vulnerability calls us to do it anyway.

In 2007, I was serving as one of the pastors at Sojourn Church in Louisville, Kentucky. We bought an old elementary school and converted it into a gathering space for our church. We also converted it into an arts center, with two art galleries, two music venues, and studio spaces. Within a few months, the 930 was flourishing, hosting Christian and non-Christian artists and housing the studios of a variety of artists, a design firm, a film-maker, and a skateboard company. We had partnerships with a local public radio station and concert promoters, and a long list of great bands (few of them "Christian") came through between 2007 and 2009: Grizzly Bear, Ingrid Michaelson, Andrew Bird, Yo La Tango, and Over the Rhine, just to name a few.

It all fell apart, though, when a local news weekly ran a front-page story about us, titled "Smells Like Holy Spirit: They're Young, Involved and Socially Aware, and Think Being Gay Is a Sin." Because the 930 was owned and operated by our church, the author of the piece—and many other folks in the community— couldn't imagine that there wasn't some "hidden agenda" in opening our doors to Louisville's arts scene. We never hid the fact that we were owned by the church, but we also never once used 930 events to try to evangelize, pass out tracts, or even suggest that people come check us out some Sunday morning. That didn't stop the author of the piece from suggesting that there were hidden motives not only to the 930 but to several local businesses owned by members of the church.

There was a tremendous backlash to the piece. Activists began a series of attacks on local blogs and posts on social media. Every time we booked a concert, people would send messages to bands and promoters saying, essentially, "You can't play there; they're a bunch of bigots." And while our partners—like the radio station and the local promoters—stood by us for a time, eventually the pressure took its toll. We booked fewer events. Attendance dropped. By 2010, we shifted our focus and almost exclusively booked Christian artists, and those only a few times a year. In 2012, we closed altogether.

Even now, I feel a tremendous amount of emotion about this experience. I look back on the 930 as a gift our church was giving to the community around us, no strings attached, and its demise breaks my heart. So many untrue things were said about us. The neighborhood lost a source of art and culture. All because we held orthodox beliefs about sexuality.

And yet—ideas have consequences, and these were the consequences of our ideas.

Recently someone asked me if, knowing what I know now, I'd launch the 930 all over again, or if I'd do something similar in the future. The answer is yes. While it lasted, the 930 *was* a gift, and it made the city a better place. If I had the opportunity to make that kind of contribution in the future, I most certainly would. It might thrive—as some similar efforts by other churches and organizations have done—or it might end exactly the same way. As I said, vulnerability calls us to do it anyway.

We don't love our cities well by withdrawing and doing

nothing. We also don't love them well if we waste our lives with political arguments about who has victimized whom. No doubt there is a need for legal battles, a need to fight for religious liberty and freedom of expression. But just as important—perhaps far more important—there is a need for the faithful witness and faithful work of Christians in culture, putting themselves at risk for the sake of others and working in ways both great and small to make their cities more peaceful, flourishing places.

CHAPTER 5

THE PLOT

ACT FIVE: ESTHER 3:6–3:15

The image of Mordecai standing alone in the crowd burned in Haman's mind. It seared the raw nerve of his hunger for power. For a person consumed by pride and power, the number of prostrate worshippers doesn't matter. The hunger that drives pride can never be satisfied, and thus the thousands don't matter; it's the one. The one standing, eyes locked, fearless of consequence, fearless of death, refusing to give him what he needed so desperately.

Haman was human. He was envious of the power of the god-king, and he'd climbed the ranks of Persia's political elite to reach a place of absolute authority. But none of these accomplishments mattered as long as Mordecai resisted.

So he plotted. He dreamed of murder. He imagined Mordecai's twisted, impaled frame hung high above the city.

And yet, he knew that even this dream wasn't enough to satisfy the hunger inside him. The rabbis describe hunger for power like having a pet crocodile. You feed it and feed it, but it's never satisfied.[1]

So he plotted further: not only did he want to see Mordecai dead, he wanted to see his entire race wiped from the face of the earth. "There's a poison in your empire," he told the king, "a scattered people who live by their own laws, worship their own God, and refuse to obey your laws."

The king's mind echoed with the memory of the recent plot, with a sense of being exposed, and with a fear of weakness in the wake of the failure of the Greek war.

Haman preyed on that fear. "Why tolerate them?" he asked. "Why let them live apart? Why trust that they will be loyal?"

This scattered people couldn't unseat the whole empire, but they could cause a great deal of trouble. They could conspire to undermine him. To erode the realm like an infection. *What might these people be capable of?*

"If you'd order it, we can destroy them. Annihilate them. Put a price on their heads, and let the people of the empire itself—their own neighbors—kill them and take their possessions, their wealth, their land."

It was a twofold win for the king: kill a cancer inside the empire; refill the empty treasuries drained by the failure in Greece.

This moment may be the reason that the name Ahasuerus—"King Headache"—is used in the Scriptures, rather than the more common "Xerxes." For starters, he never even asked who these people were. In signing the order, he unwittingly became complicit to a petty plot for revenge against Mordecai, who had saved his life not long before. Moreover, he'd signed his wife's own death warrant. But, of course, he was ignorant of all of that at the time. He was driven only by his anxiety.

There's an adage, called Godwin's law, that says any conversation on the internet, if long enough, will eventually result in someone making comparisons to Hitler. The reasons are obvious enough; Nazi Germany embodied evil in a way that is iconic. So, I must confess, I feel a bit hesitant to make that comparison here with the book of Esther. But it's unavoidable to see the parallel: We're talking about government-sanctioned attempts to exterminate the Jewish people. Exploring these two historic tragedies side by side reveals some important truths and distinctions about the nature of evil and the church's witness against it. So, bear with me; let's talk about the Nazis.

On January 20, 1942, a number of German officials gathered for what became known as the Wannsee Conference. They gathered in a dignified suburb of Berlin (called Wannsee), sat in a roomful of plush chairs and fine wooden furniture, and agreed upon the "final solution" to the "Jewish question"—the mass extermination of the Jews of Europe. It is said that the meeting was shorter than the cocktail hour that followed.

We see, here in Esther, something eerily similar. There was something so cold about the conversation. There were no arguments, no pauses, no moments of reflection or consideration. The decision didn't involve blood sacrifices or incantations to evil spirits. There was no one pounding at the gates of the palace, insisting that something must be done about these "evil Jews." Rather, the scene is quiet. Conversational. Bureaucratic, even. Timetables were set and financial gains were calculated. And with that, word was sent out to the kingdom that an entire population was to be exterminated.

Evil has many faces. It might be a reddened face in an angry mob. It might be the sadistic face of a serial killer or abuser. In Wannsee—and here, in the Persian throne room—evil wore the mask of political pragmatism. It pretended dignity. Both rooms were intoxicated by evil fantasies.

But evil has different ways of operating, seducing, and expressing itself. In this story, there's a difference between the kind of evil embodied in Haman and the evil of Xerxes. Both were complicit; both were to blame. But there's something passive about Xerxes here (and as we'll see, he was passive throughout the plot of the book of Esther) that helpfully indicates some broader truths about the way evil works in the world. This isn't to say that Xerxes wasn't an evil, brutal dictator; his campaign of terror against the virgins of Persia is akin to the terror that Haman had suggested. But when it concerns the extermination of Persian Jews, Xerxes' role was different. Knowing the difference can shape the way we bear witness against it, and it would shape the way Esther responded in the days to come.

THE EVIL OF HAMAN

At this point in the story, Haman was actively pursuing cultural change in pursuit of evil ends. He sought to shape his world in such a way that it would become darker, more vicious, more destructive to lives and souls. He was the instigator, with nakedly cruel motives. What's the proper Christian response to the Hamans of the world? Not just to their evil acts, but to the human beings themselves? They are, after all, still human beings, made in the image of God.

One possible response is a kind of empathy. We might look at Haman and say, "That could be me. There are sparks of evil, hate, and wretchedness within me that could be fanned into flames like his own." This is perfectly true, but a word of caution is needed. There's a gap between the *potential* for evil in the human heart and the *cultivation* of evil in the human heart. Haman wasn't just someone who woke up one day and gave himself over to murder and genocide. Instead, we see someone who nurtured fantasies of murder, whose appetite for power was absolute, and who allowed this darkness to flourish and grow in his imagination. What started as a personal grudge bloomed into a fantasy of genocide.

And so, while we recognize our shared humanity and our shared capacity for evil, we must also respond with fierce conviction and resistance to the type of evil Haman carried into the world. There's a common saying that "one man's terrorist is another's freedom fighter." This is exactly the kind of equivocation we must resist as people who believe in good, evil, and the dignity of humanity.

Slavoj Žižek, a political philosopher and cultural critic, discussed this temptation to equivocate acts of violence in his book *Violence*. He cited the trope, "an enemy is someone whose story hasn't been heard," and said, "There is, however, a clear limit to this procedure [of allowing the ultimate criminal to present himself as the ultimate victim]: is one also ready to affirm that Hitler was an enemy [only] because his story was not heard?" He went on to point out that figures such as Hitler and Stalin, seen by those intimate with their personal lives, could be warm and caring. But "the gap between their intimate experience and the horror of their acts was immense."[2]

We often talk about figures like these and use language such as "humanize" and "demonize." The effort to humanize them is to remind us that they're flesh and blood, just like us. All very true. But I suppose I want to make the case for a little more demonization in the world. In part, this is what it means to have a Christian imagination—a way of seeing the world that knows there are spirits at work beyond what we can see. Haman's evil, like Hitler's and Stalin's, was demonic. Satanic. And we need discerning imaginations that recognize that kind of evil when it arises.

EVIL AND FANTASIES

Figures such as Hitler, Stalin, and Haman share a common weapon in the spread of their evil intentions. Some call it ideology. It's a fantastic vision for the world that justifies the evil means necessary for accomplishing it. For Hitler, it was the fantasy of German supremacy, a master race, and a global empire. For Stalin, it was the fantasy of communism—a utopian world of economic equality and prosperity. For Haman, it was the purity and unity of the Persian Empire. In each case, the fantasy justified the tyrant's horrible means: concentration camps, pogroms, forced labor, war, and genocide.

This kind of fantasy isn't limited to the political realm, though. Fantasies and utopian dreams shape culture in all kinds of ways, and justify evil means to accomplish them.

Consider, for example, the arguments in favor of abortion.

Its justification depends on an ideology that dreams of a world of unbounded individual freedom, which we're told isn't possible without the right to terminate a pregnancy.

One of the seminal figures in the history of abortion in America is Margaret Sanger. She was an advocate of birth control as early as the 1920s, and many look to her as the pioneer of reproductive rights in the United States. The organizations she helped found were the predecessors to Planned Parenthood.

But when you look at the full range of her ideas, you discover more disturbing fantasies. Her advocacy for birth control and abortion wasn't simply about a woman's right to make decisions about her body (as the saying today goes), but about population control and eugenics. She believed most fervently in birth control for those who were poor or those she deemed unintelligent. She believed in forced sterilization. She dreamed of a world where undesirable members of society died out, a world full of a "purer" and "better" class of people.[3]

It's easy to see the darkness in all of this. But we also need to see the seduction of the fantasy: imagine a world without poverty, a world full of the best and brightest of humanity, a world where pregnancy never hindered anyone's ambitions. That dream captured the imagination of Sanger and her followers with such strength that it justified the dark practices of abortion and eugenics.

One of the ideological fantasies of a secular age is the dream of absolute tolerance. Imagine a world free of dispute, free of moralistic judgments, free of prejudice, free of shaming and guilt. A world where we're unmoored from transcendent moral categories, where each individual is liberated to seek his or her own happiness, however one might define it. The enemies of this fantasy are those who want to hold on to moral absolutes—which includes Christians who want to hold on to their orthodox beliefs. And while Christians in the United States are far from experiencing persecution for these beliefs (to my mind, persecution entails significant threat to life and limb), there is a growing pressure on Christians to either change their beliefs and accept the new "norms"—or disappear.

The common thread here—from Haman to Hitler to Sanger to secularism—is the way fantasies capture the imagination and give license to all kinds of evil. The thread stretches all the way back to Eden, to the original fantasy that man and woman might be "like God." Once captivated by the lie, the sins necessary to pursue the dream get justified.

THE BANALITY OF EVIL

Not everyone is a Haman, of course, and this is where we turn to Xerxes. Again, there's no doubt that Xerxes was capable of (and guilty of) the grand-scale evil that Haman was orchestrating. But in this particular instance, he seemed less the instigator and more the passive recipient of the lie. He was willing to accept mass murder in exchange for the fantasy of peace in the realm.

For another example, we can turn again to the Nazis and

to Adolf Eichmann, who attended the Wannsee Conference and who stood trial in Israel in 1961 for his role in orchestrating the Holocaust. He worked in the SS and managed the deportation of Jews to the concentration camps in the east. In the press and in the courtroom, he was characterized as a monster—a modern-day Haman.

Hannah Arendt, a philosopher and social theorist, attended much of the trial and came away with a very different conclusion. She was surprised by how unimpressive Eichmann was. He was not a monster; he was dull. Dim-witted, even. She coined the phrase "the banality of evil" to describe him.[4] He was an ordinary German administrator, one who went about his work with the same diligence he might have applied as a hospital administrator or an engineer. As she understood him, he was not a fanatic, nor was he a lunatic. He was, in fact, a law-abiding citizen—only in his world, obeying the law meant operating the machinery of mass murder.

One must assume that something similar was at work in the world of Persia, that when the order came out from the capital to exterminate the Jews, there were many "good Persians" who began to sharpen their knives. In some ways, I think this is easier to imagine than what transpired at Wannsee. This was a more brutal age, where violence was part of the "norms" of life. But our own age gave us Eichmann and Wannsee; we are fools if we think that this sort of radical evil is beyond our reach.

Most of us would like to believe we'd be part of the resistance if such an evil arose today. I know I'd like to believe that. But the history of the Holocaust paints a much darker picture. There were some who resisted, but most looked the other way . . . or much worse. They turned in their neighbors. They looted and burned Jewish businesses and synagogues. They gleefully bought the lie that society's ills could be cured if it could be cleansed of the presence of Jews. Or they simply cynically acted for their personal gain.

If Arendt was right about Eichmann, he wasn't so much the carrier of evil into the world as the unthinking participant in it. Not the liar, but one ready to unthinkingly accept the lie. Evil was normalized in the Third Reich, and Eichmann, like so many others, participated because he lacked the judgment—or refused the judgment—to discern and resist it. This isn't to say we should dismiss or justify his actions. (Arendt concluded her book on Eichmann with an argument for why he nonetheless deserved the death penalty for his crimes.) But this reality does challenge us to rethink how we might engage those who are so ensnared.

Let's return to the topic of abortion. From a Christian perspective, the evil of abortion isn't hard to see: Humanity is made in the image of God, who knits us together in our mother's womb, numbers our days, and knows us before we are born (Jer. 1:5; Ps. 139:16). An unborn child is a soul with intrinsic value and a right to life.

In the history of abortion, there are those who, like Haman, have nurtured a kind of evil and introduced it into the world, and there are those—like Eichmann—who have been seduced by that evil and become unthinking participants. This doesn't happen by accident. Great effort goes into normalizing abortion and insulating it inside of sterilized language. Pro-choice advocates talk not of children, but of "fetuses" and "products of conception." We don't talk about harvesting organs of aborted children (a common practice), but about "tissue donation." The head of an aborted child—often used in scientific research—is referred to as "calvarium."

This language game insulates individuals from the reality of evil that is taking place. Arendt described it well in *The Life of the Mind*. "Clichés, stock phrases, adherence to conventional, standardized codes of expression and conduct have the socially recognized function of protecting us against reality, that is, against the claim on our thinking that all events and facts make by virtue of their existence."[5] The key phrase here is "the claim on our thinking." With specially codified language around abortion, we create a gap between actions that we generally associate with horror—killing, organ harvesting, and so on—and our thinking. We don't have to think about it, and thus, we don't have to carry the weight of it.

For much of the pro-choice world, then, there is no association between the work of an abortion clinic and the value of human life. The evil of the work has been masked and normalized, and the perspective of pro-lifers seems absurd. Why are we fighting to preserve tissue? Why do we object to generously donating genetic material to scientific research? What right do we think we have to make determinations about other people's bodies?

For the average pro-choicer, then, the idea that abortion is murder makes no sense. Murder involves, to their minds, something categorically different from what takes place in the sterility of an abortion clinic. As Karen Swallow Prior has pointed out, there's a sense in which equating abortion with murder is also untrue. Abortion is legal; murder is not. And though we see things in a radically different way, our engagement with those who differ from us demands a careful use of language.[6] Prior wrote, "Referring to abortion providers as 'abortion ghouls,' clinic volunteers and workers as 'deathscorts' or 'bloodworkers,' and women who obtain abortions as 'murderers' is worse than inflammatory: it is unchristlike."[7]

Here lies the tension for Christians who want to redemptively participate in a faithless world. We must know the difference between a Haman—or a Hitler, a Stalin, a Sanger—and an Eichmann, or a run-of-the-mill advocate of any one of a host of values that run counter to our Christian convictions. Wisdom differentiates between those who weave great tapestries of lies and those who are caught in them. It calls for careful discernment, careful use of language, and careful judgment. Therein lies the key to differentiating between Haman and Xerxes. One created the fantasy. The other was captivated by it. Both participated in great evil in order to accomplish it.

Resisting the former—the Hamans of history—will be fierce and confrontational. Resisting the latter means understanding how a mind is taken captive and pursuing compassionate ways of helping them reimagine their world. The difference might be seen in the way to resist a culture of abortion. There is a political and ideological fight, and there is the much quieter work on the ground—the work of crisis pregnancy centers, free medical clinics, adoption agencies, and more. In other words, there are ideological battles, a fight in the world of ideas, where Christians work to unmask and unroot a cultural evil, and there are the more intimate human connections, where we confront souls whose minds have been captivated by a lie, and our calling is to compassionately help them reimagine their world.

FANTASIES, BABEL, AND A CHRISTIAN WORLDVIEW

There is perhaps no better argument against ideological fantasies than the story of the Bible. The world described from Genesis 3 until the book of Revelation is one marked by tragedy and imperfection. No kingdom lasts forever. No vision of utopia is accomplished. It's a vision that should make us suspicious of anyone—politicians, artists, celebrities, or pastors—who make grand, utopian promises.

I mention pastors intentionally here. There is a version of Christianity that offers similarly utopian promises. In fact, there are many versions. Some offer a vision of the perfect family and ideal marriage. Some offer health and wealth. Some offer perfect cures and peace of mind. Like any ideological fantasy, these come with a cost. If your family, health, or peace of mind aren't living up to the standards offered by those peddling the fantasy, they will tell you that the problem is you. You haven't led your family and children well, haven't cultivated enough faith, haven't sacrificed enough for the movement, or you've put your faith in something *other* than God.

The Bible itself doesn't give us these grand promises. Instead, it tells us that persevering through suffering is the pathway to Christian maturity. It shows us a Savior who suffered and apostles who were sick, jailed, beaten, shipwrecked, and publicly humiliated. The Old Testament patriarchs were drunks and adulterers. David—a man after God's own heart—could add murder to that list.

The life the Bible offers is not one safe from the tragedies of the world, but one in which God suffers with us and accompanies us through our hardships. There *is* a utopian vision in the Scriptures, a promise of a time when all things will be made new, but that promise will be fulfilled only by Jesus himself, in a time he determines, and in a way that surely—like his first coming—will surprise us all. Thus, no one should be more suspicious of idealistic fantasies than Christians.

In a similar way, we can be confident that the idealistic aspirations of others will eventually topple. This is both the blessing and the curse of Babel. In that story, humanity banded together with their own utopian vision: we will build this tower and be godlike. God's response to it was remarkable. He recognized that, because of their shared language, "nothing that they propose to do will now be impossible for them" (Gen. 11:6). So, he confused their language, made it so they couldn't understand one another, and the project failed. It's not just a curse: it's a blessing.

The world will always be made up of people who simply don't understand one another, who are incapable of coming to perfect unity, and who are incapable of joining forces to accomplish their dream of a perfect society. There will always be dissent and disagreement. There will always be confusion. There will always be differentiated perceptions. Babel shows us society coming together to attempt something great, and failing catastrophically. So does every utopian effort. There are those like the Shakers in Kentucky or the New Harmony community in Indiana who die slow deaths. There are those like Jesus People USA, who ultimately divide when secret sins surface and tear the community apart. And there are violent efforts at utopia, like Hitler's Germany, Stalin's Russia, and Mao's China, where an enormous machinery of power is used to enforce an ideology through campaigns of mass murder. These, too, will fall—just as North Korea's regime is destined to fail. Babel promises that all totalitarian and utopian efforts will eventually crumble.

This is a hopeful thing, and it shows how Babel is actually a gift for a fallen world. No matter how extensive an effort at evil is, there is always the reality that confusion will set in, resistance will rise, difference of opinion will find a voice, and, eventually, every totalitarian effort is destined to fail. Hannah Arendt saw this, too, though she pitched it a little differently. As she saw it, the hope of the world was in "natality"—the fact that new people are being born all the time, and that the introduction of new people in the world means there are always new actors and new perspectives in the world.[8]

The reality of Babel should also humble us, tempering our expectations and preventing us from being too grandiose in our aspirations. As author Andy Crouch once put it, "Beware of world changers—they have not yet learned the true meaning of sin."[9] As he sees it, the world is simply too big and too complex for us to assume that we can take on any grand projects to change it. It should warn us away from ideology and make us suspicious of anyone hawking grand solutions to the world's (or the church's) problems.

In fact, it is this grandiosity that will prove Haman's own undoing.

CHAPTER 6

THE CROSSROADS

ACT SIX: ESTHER 4

The order went out from the citadel. The Jews were to be destroyed, man, woman, and child, on the thirteenth day of the twelfth month, the month of Adar. The king and Haman celebrated. Haman had done his job, identifying the supposed threat to Xerxes' kingdom and devising a solution to the problem.

But the kingdom itself was thrown into confusion. The edict was, of course, terrifying for the Jews, who must prepare to fight or flee for their lives. That alone resulted in an empire in uproar. But apart from the instability caused by triggering a significant portion of the populace to prepare to leave or to fight, the edict was destabilizing—indeed, terrifying—for anyone else who was thoughtful about what such a decree could mean. *If Xerxes can purge a whole race of people,* they reflected, *then who's next?* His deathly power—once concentrated on the expansion of his empire—had twice been turned against his own people. First against the young girls of Persia, now against the Jews in his kingdom.

At the king's gate Mordecai heard the news of the edict. He gripped his robes with both hands and tore them open. The woven cloth stretched and split, spraying a fine dust. Tattered threads hung in the air, his skin exposed. He cried out, his heart as broken as the garments.

David rent his garments when he heard of the deaths of friends. Ezra rent his garments over the irreligion of Israel. The Persians themselves rent their garments when they were defeated in war against the Greeks. At such times, it's as though the heart itself swells with fury and sorrow and bursts out of one's robes.[1]

Mordecai went home and took them off. From a chest, he pulled out a heavy, rough garment made of goat's hair—the same cloth used to make bags for grain or spices. It irritates the skin, constantly denying a mourner comfort, numbing, or forgetting. So he wore it without anything else. He walked to the fireplace and gathered fistfuls of the grey ash, pouring them over his head, his face, his exposed shoulders. This was the practice of mourners, a way to identify with death itself.

He returned to the city like a ghost. A man driven mad by the looming promise of death. A vision of death, foreshadowing his own violent end.

He could no longer enter the king's gate—mourners weren't allowed in—but he stayed near the entrance, crying out, wailing. Crying to Yahweh, crying to Xerxes.

Word reached Esther that Mordecai was wailing outside the king's gate in ashes and sackcloth, and an exchange of messages ensued through her surrogates and servants. First, she sent clothes, hoping—whatever was wrong—he'd quiet himself, dress properly, and get back to normal life. But Mordecai refused the clothes, instead sending a written copy of the king's orders back to Esther. "She has to do something about this," he told her servant.

Mordecai waited, hopeful that he'd hear back from her—she'd approach the king, or she'd confront Haman. But she made no such promise.

"She says she can't," the servant said to Mordecai. They stood on the steps of the palace, just outside the king's gate. Around them, the business of Persia went on unabated. Mordecai watched people pass and felt each minute tick by as the day of execution approached.

"Why?" he asked.

"It's the king. He hasn't called her into his presence for

more than a month, and the law doesn't permit anyone—even her—to approach him without permission. It's a death sentence if you do, unless the king happens to have mercy."

Xerxes was not known for his mercy.

Mordecai's face grew dark. He thought of his cousin, safe in the walls of the palace, secure inside her secret identity. He knew what she knew: she could hide from the decree. Not only was she the queen; no one knew that she was Jewish. But something else had awoken inside Mordecai since he made his stand against Haman, and that something made him bold as he spoke his next words.

"Tell her, 'You might think you'll escape inside the walls of the palace. But if you refuse to help us, help will come from some other place. And you . . . you'll perish, and your father's house will perish with you.'"

The servant's eyes widened. "You want me to say that . . . to the queen?"

"Yes. And tell her, 'Maybe you've come into this position for such a time as this.'"

The servant went away. Mordecai waited. He leaned against the stone walls, looking like a beggar, unsure of what would come next. Time passed. Passersby ignored him as much as they could. He watched the sun crawl toward the western edge of Susa, another day nearly gone, another step closer to the end.

The servant returned. "'Go and gather all the Jews in the city,' she said. 'Hold a fast; don't eat or drink for three days and three nights. I'll do the same, and I'll have the women who are with me fast as well. After that, I'll go to the king. And if I perish, I perish.'"

Mordecai left at once.

ESTHER'S CROSSROADS

We arrive, at last, at Esther's crossroads. Mordecai had gone before her, refusing to bow when Haman was appointed vizier to the king. But now, as the death order loomed over the kingdom and the stakes were all the more dangerous, she was pushed to the edge and had to make a choice.

In the text, there is some ambiguity in her exchange with Mordecai. She was obviously hesitant to approach the king; it could warrant a death sentence. But Mordecai's response was almost, on its own, a veiled threat. "Do not think to yourself that in the king's palace you will escape any more than all the other Jews. *You think you'll escape this?*" he asked

To understand Esther's decision, we need to understand her real options, the first of which was silence. Escape, within the walls of the palace, was a real choice—even if Mordecai warned her against it. She was not known in the palace as a Jew, and withdrawal must have been tempting. Perhaps she hoped the storm would just pass her over. She might even have been tempted to keep Mordecai silent. She was, after all, the queen, and certainly had access to power that could silence him.

But withdrawal had another risk, and Mordecai hinted at that one as well. "For if you keep silent at this time, relief and deliverance will rise for the Jews from another place, but you and your father's house will perish." On the face of it, this is a contradictory statement. Mordecai was telling her that if she did nothing, God would still save the Jews—but he wouldn't save *her*. But if the Jews would be safe, why wouldn't Esther?

This might be the most important sentence in the entire book of Esther. It's the hinge of the story, and it's what makes the book so important to the Old Testament, so important to the Jewish people, and so important for us today.

First, the assertion was an unequivocal statement of faith by Mordecai. He was certain that God would preserve the Jewish people, a certainty that has undergirded Jewish life from the days of Abraham. Preservation was the core of God's promise to Abraham—that Abraham would miraculously have countless descendants, in spite of the absurdity of a couple in their nineties having children. Sarah laughed, and her child was named Isaac— "laughter"—because of the hilarity of God's unbreakable promises. Mordecai had embraced this fact: God will save the Jews.

But he might not save Esther: "You and your father's house will perish," he said.

He was reminding her not only of her Jewish ethnic identity but of her Jewish spiritual identity. She could not deny her place with God's people at a time of crisis without cutting herself off from it permanently. In saying, "Your father's house will perish," he was essentially telling Esther, "Your spiritual identity will have ended with your father's death. Withdraw now and be withdrawn forever."

Here, at last, Esther's two identities collide. Esther was forced to confront Hadassah, the woman bearing the name her parents had given her, and the lineage that came along with that name. Who would she be? If she was to remain Esther—by remaining silent and hoping to disappear within the safety of the palace walls—then the name Hadassah would be lost to history. Her father's line would "perish" and with it, her place among God's people.

Her self-identity had always been splintered; it could be so no more. The crisis demanded that one way or another, her life, her sense of self, and the image of herself that was projected into the world must change. To the eyes of everyone around her, Esther was a Persian. She could simply claim her Persian identity, a status none would question because of her marriage to a volatile and powerful king. Moreover, she could leverage the power and resources of the queen to protect herself: soldiers, servants, wealth, privilege. She could fight or blackmail or bribe or threaten her way out of trouble, should any arise.

In taking this path, she would depend on no one but herself, her wits, her resources. And don't forget: These were formidable. She had used them before to gain power and access within the palace. But this path would be in stark contrast to Mordecai's faith that "help for the Jews will come from another place." It would be a faithless response; Esther would be relying on nothing outside of herself to protect her. And as Mordecai reminded her, there is a price for faithlessness. She'd be cut off from her place among God's people.

Instead, Esther responded with an act of faith. She called for a fast—which is the only explicitly religious moment in the whole book—and committed herself to approaching the king. Rather than appealing to her own strength and wits, she threw herself on God's mercy. "If I perish, I perish," she said, knowing it is better to perish as one of God's people than to live apart from them. This is not to be mistaken with passivity, of course. It was a path of *action*, of taking steps that were for the good of her people, even though they put her at great personal risk. Thus, she embraced her identity as the girl with two names. Esther the queen would come to the king as Hadassah, the Jew.

We previously saw Mordecai refuse to bow to the idol of power. The threat Esther faced here was the same: a power that threatened her and wanted to bully her into silence. This power might also have tempted her to evade the crisis by virtue of her royalty. But in faith, like Mordecai, she chose a path that rejected power and embraced vulnerability. She put herself at risk for the good of the city, the good of God's people, and the good of her own soul.

THE SILENCE OF GOD

This turn is especially interesting when we think of the silence of God in the broader context. Remember: this was life in exile, after the fall of Jerusalem and the humiliation of the Jews at the hands of the Babylonians. Military conflict in the ancient world was seen not only as nation versus nation, but as god versus god. Israel's defeat, to the ancient world, was also the defeat of Yahweh.

If there was a thriving Jewish community in Susa, faithfully praying for the restoration of the Jews, we don't see them, and it doesn't seem as though Mordecai and Esther were part of it. They were in the world of Marduk and Ishtar, a world where God was definitely silent and perhaps absent altogether. His name was not spoken; Esther didn't even say it when she called for the fast. I think that's intentional on the part of the book's author. He wanted to make sure we see the silence of God and the absence of his name throughout the book.

Perhaps Esther dared not speak his name because she knew how far she had allowed herself to wander from his laws. Perhaps she dared not speak it because she feared he may not in fact show up. Whatever the case, it is yet one more way that God appears absent.

It's a silence familiar to God's people in ways both large and small. Where was God when Hurricane Harvey struck Houston? When cancer struck a spouse? When the Twin Towers fell? When a cloud of depression set up residence in your heart and mind, and nothing seemed able to drive it away?

It's a silence the protagonist endured for most of the book of Job. It's a silence that Mother Teresa is said to have suffered for most of her life. A silence and absence that plagued the priest and writer Brennan Manning.

Imagine this story from a different perspective—that of a faithful Jew in Susa. Perhaps you knew that Esther was a Jew, perhaps not. You've spent your life in exile, watched your friends and neighbors struggle against assimilation, suffered the anti-Semitism that seems to be alive and well in Persia (given the readiness of the Persians to take up Xerxes' and Haman's decree), and received your death sentence. Suddenly, a Jew named for a foreign god shows up and says, "We have only one hope: the queen"—a secret Jew who, you learn, has married the very tyrant who threatens you now, a girl who everyone knows must have compromised everything to be where she is. *This* girl is going to plead for your life with the king?

It might seem like yet one more humiliation. It most certainly would seem like dim hope to the Jews.

And yet, this, the book of Esther tells us, is how God sometimes shows up. *In* the silence. *In* absence. *In* the darkness of doubt, humiliation, and loss. In the most unlikely ways possible, the miracle of grace manifests.

It is precisely God's hiddenness that makes this story so hopeful. Whatever dark place you are in today, whether by hapless circumstance or by your own actions, God hasn't forgotten you. Esther's story invites us to cling to hope, however small, and to confidence that whatever evil might currently reign, the story of God isn't finished.

VULNERABILITY AND CYNICISM

There's a kind of cynicism that keeps the world at arm's length and insulates us from the pain of disappointment and the frustration of failure. Being cynical is kind of a cure-all for disappointment: *Of* course *things didn't turn out well; we never expected anything different.*

In this part of our story, Esther herself flirted with cynicism, and Mordecai frightened her away from it.

It began with the rending of Mordecai's robes. This was a violent and passionate image: threads bursting, knuckles white against fabric, body exposed. Tearing garments was a common expression of mourning, and in some circles of Jewish life today, it's still practiced. It's called *kriah*, and it's done more subtly now. A mourner tears a black ribbon in the presence of a deceased person, and wears the torn ribbon for a period of time, as long as thirty days. It is an image of brokenness, of irreparability, and of poverty. Clothes—especially for someone of influence, like Mordecai—were expensive, and tearing them ruined them.

So, upon hearing the order of death to the Jews, Mordecai tore his clothes like a mourner at a funeral, exposed his body, and then clothed himself with ashes and sackcloth—the clothes of the very poorest. He was the embodiment of death.

Not only was Mordecai exposed as a Jew, he was exposed as one marked for death. And he exposed his own sorrow. He poured his heart out, and he did so without the promise of someone coming along and celebrating him for his bravery and vulnerability. He would, instead, be ostracized, banned from the king's gate, and would embarrass those like Esther, who knew him. No one would say, "How brave of you! Thanks for sharing." There was nothing to be gained. His was a display that weakened him—embracing the real risk of vulnerability—rather than strengthened him.

This kind of weakness takes courage. One wonders if we have courage enough to be passionate before the world today. Are we courageous enough to weep with those who weep? To laugh with those who laugh? Are we willing to *feel* something in a world that rewards being distracted and unfeeling?

THE PARADOX OF WEAKNESS

People have made an entire career of their so-called vulnerability. They tell embarrassing, humiliating stories about themselves, stories about bad decisions, abuse, and addiction, and they are lauded for their bravery. This practice seems to come primarily from two very different platforms: that of the stand-up comic, and that of the preacher.

For each, his or her "vulnerability" is something to be leveraged. Comedians like Mike Birbiglia and Amy Schumer, as well as comedy writers like Lena Dunham, tell humiliating stories about themselves as a way to win over the audience. Richard Pryor pioneered this approach to comedy, telling stories about the sexual, physical, and verbal abuse he endured as a child.

Doing so, Pryor said, enabled you to decide *why* people laughed at you. It put you in control and was a way to take back a certain kind of power.

The same experience is possible in the pulpit. Pastors can share their stories of suffering, humiliation, and spiritual struggles in a way that elicits deep sympathy, actually leveraging the experiences they relate to endear themselves to their audience.

Social media also invites this kind of openness. We can go online and share stories about disastrous relationships, parenting "fails," and moments of public humiliation in a way that, again, endear us to the watching world.

To be sure, something redemptive exists in this kind of self-disclosure, and I'm not out to shut it down. But if we're honest, we have to admit that in each of these situations, there's actually nothing really at risk. Richard Pryor may have taken risks sharing his stories, but forty years later it's an established part of the art of comedy.

What we're talking about here is what a friend once referred to as "openness," something that looks like vulnerability but actually contains no real *risk*. The comic, the pastor, and the social-media poster can all use these experiences to prop themselves up. They are "brave" and "courageous" for exposing their failures and their dark sides, but the context is actually a safe one. It's akin to what I've said already about victimhood: openness is a lever for a certain kind of power and influence.

Consider the difference, for example, between a pastor in the pulpit talking about struggles with parenting and a pastor in his study telling a close friend how racked with disappointment he is in his own capacities as a dad. In the first example, there's much to gain: He's seen as an "ordinary guy," and his credibility as a teacher is heightened. His failures become an object lesson and are useful for his other goals. The risk, if there is any, is mild: he might stir the ire of a few of the church's strictest Pharisees, but no pastor really cares what those people think anyway.

On the other hand, if in the privacy of his study he shares the exact same thing one-on-one with a trusted friend, everything about the conversation is different. Not only does he expose his weakness, he invites deeper exposure. He invites further questions that may reveal more than he intends. He risks judgment and rejection. What he gains, though, is different too. He gains the opportunity for real intimacy and real communion.

This distinction is important to consider as we watch Mordecai rip his robes open and expose his chest. It could easily be confused for the kind of grandstanding "openness" that is all-too-familiar in the age of platform building and social media. But in Mordecai's case, there wasn't going to be an adoring crowd standing in the wings, ready to celebrate him for his courage. Instead, there was a legion of Persians, sharpening their knives. Mordecai's grand gesture involved real risk to life and limb, and it was driven by conscience, not by a desire to sway the opinion of the crowd. It was simultaneously a gesture of weakness and courage, vulnerability and strength.

Courage and vulnerability are twins willing to run headlong into danger because it's the right thing to do.

CHOOSING BETWEEN DEATH AND DEATH

In the opening lines of the *Inferno*, Dante wrote:

> At the mid-point of the path through life, I found
> Myself lost in a wood so dark, the way
> Ahead was blotted out. The keening sound
> I still make shows how hard it is to say
> How harsh and bitter that place felt to me—
> Merely to think of it renews the fear—
> So bad that death by only a degree
> Could possibly be worse. As you shall hear,
> It led to good things eventually.[2]

It is, perhaps, the world's most famous midlife crisis. It is also most likely the worst. Dante is exiled from his hometown of Florence, fearing for his life, and longing for his one true love. He finds himself alone and lost in a dark wood, and comes to the realization that the only way out of his circumstances and misery is through it. It's a realization that leads him not only through the woods, but into the mouth of hell itself, descending deeper and deeper and observing countless tortures, through the pain of purgatory, and eventually, to redemption. The message of *The Divine Comedy* is clear: The pathway *out* of darkness is *through* darkness. And it might get worse before it gets better.

It is at just such a crossroads where we find Esther. She must either enter the dark woods and face death itself, or remain lost, aimless, and detached. She faced a choice between the pain of a numbed, soulless life and the pain of death that might result from her courage. This is the most important moment in her story, and it's the one that is the most challenging for each of us.

Life in the citadel, especially life in the palace itself, was much like life in our own world. It was a place of comfort and distractions. A place in which a person could lose herself in entertainment and gossip. And while most of us aren't surrounded by servants and golden goblets, a life full of distractions is universal. We can lose ourselves in headphones and smartphones, in mindless consumption of television, in endless meals of empty calories, in shopping, in bickering about politics, in sense-dulling drugs and drinks, and in much, much more. In a world shadowed by the prospect of death, we have to constantly face the temptation to lose ourselves in anything else, to avoid the pain. To break out of such a life, one has to recognize that, really, it isn't life at all. It is a certain kind of death, a numbness that not only masks our pain but insulates us from joy.

Esther's choice is therefore one between death and death: a death defined by courage and a willingness to sacrifice on behalf of others, or a death defined by numbness and withdrawal. Only one path—the path of risk—offers deep satisfaction and real life.

In a lecture by Brené Brown, she asked an audience to react to a scene.[3] She described it as an opening scene in a movie—a family packing up joyfully for a day at the beach. They pack their coolers, their swimsuits, their sunscreen, their beach chairs and umbrellas, and excitedly get in the family car for the drive to the beach. If this is a movie, she asks, what do we expect to happen next?

Almost universally, members of the audience described a tragedy. Someone gets sick in the car. A fight breaks out between the husband and wife. A Mack truck obliterates them. In contrast, what seems hard for the audience to imagine is the family going to the beach and having a nice day together. The point is this: We are suspicious of joy. It opens us up to the possibility of disappointment. It invites pain because it brings us to a precipice, and it makes it possible to fall all the further and all the harder.

Yet this suspicion isn't natural. It is formed in us by the experiences of frustration, disappointment, and pain. Our hopes are raised and dashed, and throughout our lives we collect scars from these experiences. The natural response to pain is to think, *I won't do that again*, and that's a perfectly good response to being burned on the stove or bitten by a strange dog. But in much of life, it's an unnatural response. Relationships aren't supposed to be marked by pain. Social life isn't supposed to be an accumulation of scars. It's simply not the way the world was meant to be, and when we let those experiences lead us to be suspicious of joy, we are allowing ourselves to be formed into creatures who are cynical enough to never be surprised by pain, but closed off from the world and robbed of joy.

When we run from pain and numb ourselves to the world, we foster this cynicism. We set joy at a distance because we've determined that the possibility of joy isn't worth the risk of disappointment. When we're pain avoidant, we're joy avoidant. And a joyless life is no life at all.

Esther's story illustrates this in bold, dramatic strokes. Terrible pain awaited her people, and one option she had was simply to look the other way and retreat from it. But Mordecai told her that if she did nothing, she would still perish. She'd be lost in the numbness of the palace, in the knowledge of her failure to act, in a life cut off from the blessing that comes from being known as one of God's people.

The only real option is to see the dark wood and enter it. The only way out of suffering is through it. We have to open ourselves to the possibilities of pain, failure, and heartache if we want to experience the goodness of joy, thriving, belonging, and redemption.

CHAPTER 7

THE THRONE ROOM

ACT SEVEN: ESTHER 4:16-5:5

Esther gathered her closest allies and confessed her secret. She asked them to fast with her—to fast *for* her—as she prepared to risk her life and appear before the king.

For three days, they fasted. Esther herself took no food or water. Her fears robbed her of sleep. She shrank in frame as hunger and dehydration set in. Her eyes hollowed; her skin paled; her posture sank from weakness and weariness. She embraced and embodied suffering.

The third day came, and she steadied herself for the challenge ahead. Her chambermaids dressed her in her royal robes, somber, fearing that they may never see her again. She left her chambers and entered the palace, crossing a wide courtyard with cobbled steps. Banners waved above the palace towers and the king's gate. Guards and officials shuffled about, some startled at the sight of the weary queen.

Xerxes' throne room was a massive hall. At its entrance a curtain ran the full height of the chamber, with guards at either side and others standing nearby. Esther watched a eunuch exit the chamber, leaving for some official business. She approached the guards.

"I need to see the king."

"Have you been summoned?"

Esther was silent.

"You know the law."

"I know the law."

The guards looked at one another. They looked at the shrunken queen. One reached up and slid the curtain open, and the queen entered.

At the far end of the throne room, the king's throne sat atop a pedestal, high above the advisors who gathered around him. Their chatter echoed dimly in the empty, enormous room. Torchlight animated the painted reliefs along the walls, so as Esther passed them, images of violence and power moved about her. It seemed as though the carvings noticed her before the officials did.

She neared the throne and the conversations ahead of her gradually died. She was met by stunned eyes, officials nearly recoiling in fear at the sight of the queen breaking the law of the land. She arrived at the edge of the pedestal, her eyes down. The king stared at her—her downcast eyes, her slumped shoulders, her frame sunken into her robe.

When she looked up, she saw the king descending the stairs, extending his scepter—a sign that he was showing her mercy. His face wasn't angry, but saddened, even hor-rified, at the sight of his broken queen.

She touched the end of the scepter and knew that her life had been spared.

"What is it, my queen?" he said, taking her hand and leading her up the steps, where he then took his seat again on his throne. "Ask anything of me and I'll give it. Even half of my kingdom."

"If it would please you, I want to prepare you a feast."

The king paused, curious. So dramatic a gesture for such a simple request. He sat back, cocked his head, try-ing to comprehend his broken queen. "Of course," he said. "Anything you ask."

She bowed and turned to leave. Paused, turned back.

"And bring Haman."

The king summoned Haman at once.

A VISION OF DEATH

Esther's entry into the king's chamber is a moment the Sunday school version of the story tends to get wrong. In that version, Esther's appearance in the throne room is a moment that evokes the king's great love for her and arouses his great admiration for her beauty. That may be true, but the emphasis there is misleading. Esther didn't come in radiance, but in brokenness and desolation.

In a midrash—a Jewish commentary on the book of Esther— Esther's three days in fasting are compared to the three days that Jonah spent in the belly of a fish. They're also connected to the three days of agony that Abraham spent believing he'd have to kill Isaac. Redemption, the midrash tells us, comes on the third day.[1]

But let's not rush to the redemption just yet, because those three days deserve our attention. They were a time of torment and agony. Abraham's burden must have left him sleepless and weary. Jonah's days inside a fish surely turned him into a horrific vision. I doubt he emerged unscathed. I imagine him bruised and tattered, his skin inflamed from all the horrible things happening inside a fish's digestive tract. When Jonah arrived at Nineveh, he didn't just proclaim God's wrath—he embodied it: a horrifying vision of suffering and death.

Esther the queen retreated into the palace for three days and took no food or water, and it was only then—hungry, wearied, dehydrated—that she approached the king. He was not moved simply by her beauty, but by her anguish. "What is it, Queen Esther?" he asked. What could possibly have made her so downcast, and yet so bold as to enter into his presence unbidden and potentially invoke the wrath such brazenness invited?

Paul wrote to the Corinthians, "God chose what is weak in the world to shame the strong" (1 Cor. 1:27). Our story is reaching a fever pitch here, as Esther voluntarily descended into weakness, in contrast with the rising fury and conniving power of Haman. The murderous power of empire was boring in upon her, and the girl with two names put her life on a collision course with it.

Esther gives us both a way of life to follow—a pathway defined by *choosing* weakness over strength—and a signpost to follow. She leads and she points to another who became obedient even to death.

In another midrash, it's said that Esther spent her three days meditating on the opening verse of Psalm 22. On the first day, she prayed, "My God." On the second, "My God." And on the third, "Why have you forsaken me?" It is the same psalm that Jesus cried out on the cross.

The way of Esther is the way of the cross.

AWAKENING TO VISION

Mordecai awakened Esther from her complacency by reminding her of who she was. He gave her a vision that made it possible for her to snap out of her comfort and apathy. She is her father's daughter. She belongs to her father's people. This vision gave her the courage and resolution to risk her life, and, frankly, it's the only thing that could have.

When I think about where we are today, in a world gone mad, I cannot help but think that our only real hope is some kind of revelation. A fresh vision of what it means to be God's people. Too often, that's been defined by the shallow veneer of cultural Christianity.

To be sure, there are many versions of that veneer. There is the contemporary consumer version, where "the good life" is embodied by young, energetic pastors shouting from stages full of lights, smoke, and fancy backdrops. There are politicized versions of it, where holy water is thrown on ideologies left and right. And there are a dozen other varieties.

These "tribes" exist within the church, and belonging to any one of them comes with a certain set of rules. In each case, the vision of the good life is defined by being "right," and the common thread is the way each one is a veneer, a thin surface that's meant to please the eyes and conceal the depths. Each one provides us a way to *perform* our faith in public. We want to be seen as orthodox/compassionate/relevant, and each one has evolved into a little world of its own, in which we can perform the rites of membership. We go to the right churches, read the right books, vote the right way in elections, share the right hashtags, buy the right T-shirts, consume the right food and goods, all as ways of signaling our belonging.

Rather than being *primarily* formed and united by a Christian vision of life, we seek membership in any one of these tribes, each of which has its own wholly secular counterpoints. And here's where this point becomes most important: if we find that we have more in common with our secular tribal counterparts than with our Christian brothers and sisters who hold differing political views or belong to some other subculture, then something has gone terribly wrong.

These identities are somewhat prepackaged for Christians and non-Christians alike, for conservatives and liberals. It's a powerful temptation to simply conform to the norms of any given tribe; it answers myriad questions that the soul is asking and provides a sense of rootedness (liberating you from the burden of having to *think* about what you believe).

But as I said, it's only a veneer. As powerful a temptation as one of these veneered expressions of identity might be, they all fail to ultimately satisfy. They're powerful enough to change the patterns of your life, but they fail to answer the big questions being asked by the soul. That's why our world seems perpetually on a quest for something else. You see it in our consumer culture, in our politics, in the restlessness and impermanence of interpersonal relationships, in the low-grade dissatisfaction most people feel in their jobs. There's an aching sense that something more is out there.

By warning Esther of the end of her father's lineage, Mordecai called her back to a deeper vision of belonging—membership in the community of God's people and the inheritance of God's promise. It was a call away from her own veneered identity—the life of Esther, named for Ishtar, living among the Persians—and into a deeper identity and a deeper belonging as Hadassah.

This is the question we should be asking ourselves: What world do we want to belong to? In an age when faith is contested at all times, when meaning and purpose evade us, where the only thing our culture can provide us is the veneer of tribal signaling and consumerism, we need an awakening. We need a better way, a deeper way, a deeper stream of identity and purpose. And when we awaken to the deeper stream of belonging that comes from being God's child, we awaken to love.

COMING HOME

There once was a father who had two sons. The younger became intoxicated with a vision of life far from home—a life in the city, a life of sex and money and indulgence, a life chasing the goddess of pleasure—and so he asked for his inheritance early. It was a dishonor to the whole family. But the father let him have it. Perhaps it was a strange grace; rather than force him to live out his disgrace among the family, he gave the son his money and let him go his way.

But life away from home was a disaster. Pleasure is a fickle goddess, and her blessings are withdrawn as quickly as they're given. The young man spent more and more in pursuit of her, until he found himself empty, broke, and destitute. He took a disgraceful job tending pigs—which, as a Jew, was doubly disgraceful—eventually eating with them.

Then, he had an awakening. He wanted to go home. This wouldn't be simple, and it wouldn't be joyful. It meant returning to his disgrace and facing the deep shame and humiliation of his failures. He had been so wrong about so many things. He had caused irreparable rifts between himself and his father, and himself and his brother. And yet he wondered if, nevertheless, they might take him on as a servant. Better to be the lowliest person in his father's house than to live another day in the filth, far from it.

So, he began the journey homeward, rehearsing a speech he'd make, begging for a job among his father's laborers.

While he was still a long way off, his father saw him and came running to him, greeting him before he could barely begin his speech. A robe was brought. A signet ring. And shoes. A feast was prepared. And as the celebration began, one person stood outside it—the elder brother, who couldn't comprehend the lavish generosity of the father. He wouldn't enter the feast.[2]

ESTHER AS PRODIGAL

Esther's story is the story of a prodigal, far from home, assimilated into a world where she didn't belong, who had an awakening. Make no mistake, life among the pleasures of the palace is no different from life among the pigs—at least, not after you've awoken to the reality of the kingdom of God.

Which, really, is what happened to Esther. She had the choice of being counted among the Persians or counted among the Jews, and once she remembered who she was, there was no turning back. As the psalmist says, "I would rather be a doorkeeper in the house of my God than dwell in the tents of wickedness" (Ps. 84:10). Better to die as one of God's people than to live as the queen of Persia. *If I perish, I perish.*

Jesus told the story of the prodigal son in the midst of a series of parables, each one serving to offend the Pharisees in his audience. They raised their objections and sneered at him, accusing him of playing too easy and light with the law. His response, though, was to certify himself as fully committed to the law. And yet, a new era—or perhaps better put, a new revelation—was upon them:

> "The Law and the Prophets were proclaimed until John. Since that time, the good news of the kingdom of God is being preached, and everyone is forcing their way into it." (Luke 16:16 NIV)

There's a similar statement made in Matthew 11:12, where Jesus describes how the kingdom of God suffers violence, "and the violent take it by force."

The prodigal son and Esther were among the violent, who awakened to a vision of belonging and threw themselves upon it. And the Pharisees couldn't stand it. Like the elder brother, they couldn't comprehend the injustice of a God who would let the son come home. Neither could they comprehend Esther, if they really looked at her story.

How could someone who was so deeply compromised, and who had so profoundly abandoned her roots with the people of God, so readily attempt to count herself among them? How could she pretend she had a place with them? Even worse, how could she become a hero of the faith?

It's why people don't deal honestly with Esther. In Jewish and Christian commentaries alike, we see her story whitewashed. She's painted as secretly virtuous, a Daniel in disguise, in spite of evidence to the contrary.

And yet the mercy of God is evident in her story and in the place she takes in Jewish history. Esther didn't just come home; she came home to a feast. She became a hero.

The mercy of God shines brightest when prodigals come home. When Esther said, "If I perish, I perish," she came home.

ESTHER THE SIGNPOST

Stories shift and move as they are examined from different perspectives. They're like a fabric whose threads weave and cross and stretch, appearing different as we turn them over in our hands and trace the textures of their surfaces.

Esther's story has this quality, for it not only demonstrates how prodigals come home, but it also provides a signpost for why the Father welcomes them. "If I perish, I perish" is the refrain both of someone who's had an awakening and someone who's willing to give her life for another.

In this way, Esther points us to Jesus. As Paul described him, Jesus,

> Who, being in very nature God,
> did not consider equality with God something to be
>   used to his own advantage;
> rather, he made himself nothing
> by taking the very nature of a servant,
> being made in human likeness.
> And being found in appearance as a man,
> he humbled himself
> by becoming obedient to death—
> even death on a cross!
>
> (PHIL. 2:6–8 NIV)

Esther's journey to the throne room mirrors this journey of Jesus, in which his equality with God entitled him to all of the honor, glory, and dignity of life in the palace of heaven, but who laid it aside for the redemption of his people. To say, "If I perish, I perish" is to walk in the way of the cross.

Consider how closely Esther's journey followed Jesus' own.[3] She entered a throne room no one else could rightfully enter, and she invited the king's wrath in order to protect others from it. Jesus did the same. And just as the Jews were saved because Esther embraced death, so are we saved by Jesus, who did the same. Again, "God chose the foolish things of the world to shame the wise; God chose the weak things of the world to shame the strong" (1 Cor. 1:27 NIV). Esther's embrace of weakness shamed the strength of Haman. Her act of humiliation overcame his exercise of power.

The book of Hebrews describes Jesus' work of redemption as that of the ultimate high priest. In the Jewish temple, only the high priest could enter the Most Holy Place, the throne room, so to speak, where God's presence dwells. To do so without God's invitation—without observing the rules of entry and performing all the cleansing rites and rituals—was to face the punishment of death. Sinners cannot just stroll into the presence of a holy God, who is elsewhere described as a consuming fire (Deut. 4:24; Heb. 12:29).

Jesus entered the throne room of God's presence on behalf of God's people, and he carried their sins on his back. He then suffered the consequences on our behalf, and made a way for the rest of us to "boldly" enter in after him (Heb. 4:16 KJV).

Esther, like Jesus, entered a throne room and welcomed death on behalf of God's people, and her selfless act likewise preserved their lives.

In Esther's case, her life was a movement from compromise to conviction. She had the wealth, power, and beauty that many of us believe will make us happy. Her compromise was her means of accumulating power; likewise, we compromise our own convictions, desires, and preferences in exchange for something we want—power, prestige, cultural influence, or something else. To make the opposite choice, to sacrifice power for the sake of our convictions, is difficult and painful.

But this is our holy invitation in a world gone mad. Jesus said, "Whoever does not take his cross and follow me is not worthy of me. Whoever finds his life will lose it, and whoever loses his life for my sake will find it" (Matt. 10:38–39). It's a choice between death and death—the soul-destroying death of numbness and self-interest, or the death to self that comes from giving our lives away to others. We follow Esther, and, moreover, we follow Jesus on a pathway that allows for real risk in our homes, our relationships, and in our cities, entering a world of death and decay and bringing, in our own deaths, flourishing and life.

CHAPTER 8

THE FEASTS, THE HONOR, AND THE DOWNFALL

ACT EIGHT: ESTHER 5-9

What happened next in Esther's story is a bit like watching a Rube Goldberg machine—one of those elaborate contraptions where one drops a ball down a chute, which spins a wheel, which turns a pulley, which sends a domino falling onto a lever, and on it goes until, at the end, it captures a mouse, or starts a car, or performs some other task.

In this case, each event triggered another. Esther's risk is the trigger, and what unfolds is the downfall of Haman, the rise of Mordecai, and the redemption of God's people.

The feast was splayed out on tables. It was abundant. Extravagant. The king and Haman ate together and drank wine, and the queen and her attendants saw to their every need. Course after course was laid before them. And yet, Esther remained anxious, frail.

The evening grew quiet. The king studied the weary face of the queen. "What is it, Esther? What do you need? Ask for anything."

She paused, eyeing Haman. Finally, she said, "If it pleases the king, let me prepare another feast for you and Haman tomorrow night. Then I'll make my request."

The king agreed, the party dispersed, and Haman left for home, his spirits high from the honor of sitting at the king's table at the request of the queen. He passed through the palace courtyards, guards and servants bowing as he passed. He walked through the king's gate and turned to the long stair leading away from the palace and into the citadel, and there he found Mordecai.

Mordecai, still in sackcloth and ashes. Still a vision of death. Still refusing to kneel before the king's vizier. Their eyes met, Haman's murderous, Mordecai's defiant. And wordless, they parted.

At home, Haman flew into a rage. This Jew's refusal to show proper honor was all it took to unravel all that he had accomplished. His wife watched as he shouted and threw cups, smashed jars, seethed.

"Make an example of him," she said. "Hang him high on a stake, high as any ever built. Watch him flail, die, and wither, and let the whole kingdom see what happens to those who refuse to honor Haman."

He turned to a servant and ordered the work to begin, a stake seventy-five feet high, to be built for Mordecai the Jew.

The king was awake, unable to sleep. He worried for his queen. He worried for his kingdom. When he'd banished Vashti, he'd been humiliated, and he couldn't stand the idea of being humiliated again. He worried now that some ill fate had befallen Esther, and feared what might come about as a result.

He wandered into his throne room, sent for the palace scribes, and asked that the chronicles of his recent history be read. Perhaps he wanted them read to feed his fragile ego, hearing once again of his exploits and great deeds. Perhaps he read looking for some clue as to why the queen was so disturbed, and why his own spirit was so restless.

The chronicles were read deep into the night. Eventually, they came upon the story of Bigthan and Teresh, the king's servants who'd plotted against him. Mordecai's name was read—the informant who'd saved the life of the king.

Xerxes sat up. "What's been done to honor this man?" It was important, in a kingdom like Persia, to reward loyalty to those who'd served the king.

The king's servant scanned the pages. "Nothing," he said. It was nearly dawn.

Haman rose early the next day, red-eyed and weary after a sleepless night of simmering rage. He dressed and made his way through the citadel as the sun came up and the city began to stretch and yawn and begin its business.

He rehearsed a speech in his head, a speech about his own exploits, the rights he'd earned, his faithful service to the king, all of it a preamble to the request he was at last ready to make: He wanted to kill Mordecai the Jew. It couldn't wait until the day of the edict.

He was surprised to find the king awake, at his throne, looking as weary and worse for wear as he himself did after a sleepless night. Haman opened his mouth to speak, but was immediately cut off by the king.

"Haman," the king said, "what should be done for a man the king delights to honor?"

Haman stood speechless for a moment. *Who in the kingdom would Xerxes want to honor more than me?* he thought. *Surely, that is his intent.*

He pictured the city streets, the throngs of people who already had to bow to him. How else could he be shown powerful among them? He thought of the king's robes— said to contain the blessing and power of the gods. Finally, he answered.

"Bring him a robe and a crown. One that you've worn. Put him on one of your own horses—one you've actually ridden— and assign one of your highest-ranking princes to lead the horse through the streets, announcing to all who hear, 'This is what the king does for the man he delights to honor.'"

The king listened and watched closely. He realized that Haman was thinking of himself, and began to understand that Haman may not be such a benevolent servant. He looked, instead, like a hungry crocodile with an appetite for power. He smiled as Haman spun up his vision of honor, watching him build a trap for his own ego.

At last, Haman finished. "Good," said Xerxes. "Go at once and find Mordecai, the Jew. Let everything be done for him just as you say, and you yourself should lead the horse through the city."

A long, silent moment passed. Haman grasped for the words of his request, which he never got near asking. He couldn't imagine a worse outcome. And yet, there was nothing to do but obey the king.

He left the throne room and sent for Mordecai, then grudgingly carried out everything just as he had said. He led the horse through the city, and a bewildered Mordecai towered over him, dressed in the king's robes. "This is what the king does for the man he delights to honor," Haman shouted, miserably. It was a refrain he said again and again as he walked up and down the streets of Susa, and the people shouted and cheered or knelt in honor of this man whom, apparently, the king wanted to ensure was honored.

In the evening, he returned Mordecai to his home. Then Haman returned the horse to the palace, wrapped himself in a cloak, and covered his head to hide from the crowds as he walked home.

By the time he got there, the sun had set. The stake had been built, and it sat in the dusky shadows like a brooding monster.

He entered his house, but tonight, there was no rage—just defeat. His wife watched him as he unwrapped his cloak and collapsed on a cushion in the corner of the room.

"This Mordecai," she said, "is he Jewish?"

Haman nodded.

A long silence passed between them.

"You're done," she said at last.

A knock came just then, at the door. The king's servants were there, ready to take him to the queen's banquet.

The second feast was just as lavish as the first. The queen and her servants attended to the king and Haman as they reclined at the table. The scent of roasted meat, rare spices, and the boozy smell of wine hung thickly in the air. They ate until late into the evening, and Haman's spirits were brightened, at least a bit, by the heavy meal.

At the end of the evening, the king implored Esther again: "What's wrong? Why this show of desperation and extravagance?"

"If I've found any favor with you, and if you'd grant it, spare my life," she cried, "and spare my people! We've been sold, all of us, to be wiped out by the people of Persia!

"If we'd merely been enslaved and had our lives spared, I would have kept silent," she went on. "But our lives hang in the balance!"

The king was shocked. He genuinely had no idea what she was talking about. He stared for a long time at his queen, who stood silent, head bowed, trembling.

"How has this happened? Who has caused all of this?"

"Our enemy," she said, pointing an accusing finger, "is Haman!"

Haman's eyes grew wide, terrified, and as confused as the king's. Then the revelation sank in: *Queen Esther is Jewish.*

Xerxes stormed from the room, overwhelmed with rage. Haman threw himself at Esther's feet, shouting an incoherent chorus of pleas for mercy. When the king returned and saw him gripping Esther's garments, his rage overflowed.

"You'd attack her now? Here? In my own home?"

Haman was speechless. The air hung with tension. Esther dared not speak.

One of the eunuchs approached the king, quietly. "You know," he said, "Haman recently built a very large stake . . ."

Haman was impaled on the stake and hung high above the city (7:10 NIV). His household and all his possessions were given to Esther, who handed them over to Mordecai. The king also gave Mordecai his signet ring—a symbol of power and authority. Then the king's advisors were brought back to the throne room, and Haman's reign came to an end.

But the death sentence still hung over the Jews. A month passed. Then another. Finally, Esther took it upon herself to once again enter the throne room unbidden and throw herself at the king's mercy. She fell at his feet, and he once again extended his scepter and spared her life. Then she pleaded once again for the lives of the Jews.

There were legal problems, though. An edict from the king couldn't be rescinded. So instead, a new edict was written—this time to the Jews directly, ordering them to take up arms and defend themselves against anyone who would plan to attack them. Couriers spread word from one end of Persia to the other, and when the day came—the thirteenth day of the month of Adar, the day when the Jews were to be annihilated at Haman's treacherous command, the reverse happened. Anyone who hated the Jews and dared take up arms was killed. In Susa itself, that included five hundred people on the thirteenth, and another three hundred the next day, the fourteenth. Among the captured were Haman's ten sons, who were impaled on spikes on the second day.

In the end, the day meant for the destruction of the Jews became a day of redemption. They killed more than seventy-five thousand of their would-be assailants, yet they took none of their property (which would have been theirs by the rights afforded in the law), and the kingdom fell into a new realm of peace and a time of safety and security for the Jews.

GIVING HAMAN HIS DUE

Haman's crocodile finally grew too large, too hungry, and turned on its master. This is why Haman didn't die of old age in the comfort of the palace. His appetite for power flared when it was confronted by the unflinching resistance of Mordecai, inspiring him to erect the stake that ultimately took his own life.

Now, this may sound odd, but I want to take a moment to make sure we avoid overemphasizing God's hand in Haman's fate. Don't get me wrong: God is sovereign over all of these events, and he orchestrated them for the redemption of his people. The

Jews were far more secure when the battle was over than they were at the beginning of the book, and it seems certain that this was God's plan all along.

But responsibility for Haman's downfall lay with Haman. His grandiose vision led him to presume that the king would want to honor him above all his other subjects. It also led to his resentment of Mordecai and the building of a spectacular, seventy-five-foot stake. Those who resisted his spectacular authority, he thought, deserved a spectacular death. Yet it was he, not Mordecai, who became the spectacle.

Grasping for power—like grasping for *anything*—will ultimately lead to self-destruction. That thing we grasp for, that thing we've deluded ourselves into believing holds the key to making us ultimately and spectacularly happy—it cannot be held on to, and it will ultimately eat you alive.

David Foster Wallace spoke of this in his famous Kenyon College commencement speech, "This Is Water."

In the day-to-day trenches of adult life, there is actually no such thing as atheism. There is no such thing as not worshipping. Everybody worships. The only choice we get is what to worship. And the compelling reason for maybe choosing some sort of god or spiritual-type thing to worship—be it JC or Allah, be it YHWH or the Wiccan Mother Goddess, or the Four Noble Truths, or some inviolable set of ethical principles—is that pretty much anything else you worship will eat you alive. If you worship money and things, if they are where you tap real meaning in life, then you will never have enough, never feel you have enough. It's the truth. Worship your body and beauty and sexual allure and you will always feel ugly. And when time and age start showing, you will die a million deaths before they finally grieve you. . . . Worship power, you will end up feeling weak and afraid, and you will need ever more power over others to numb you to your own fear. Worship your intellect, being seen as smart, you will end up feeling stupid, a fraud, always on the verge of being found out.[1]

Haman's foolishness is the foolishness of all idolatry. It is feasting on ashes, as Isaiah 44:20 says, a vain and empty attempt at satisfaction that is, in reality, poisonous.

It's important that we acknowledge that Haman was responsible for his fate, even while we marvel at God's hand in orchestrating the sequence of events that make up the plot of Esther. Haman's story isn't that he was a pawn in the hands of a clever (and perhaps malevolent) God; it's that the idol of power is self-destructive. God *used* that self-destructive power in a way that redeemed and protected God's people. But this is no more an endorsement of the love of power than it is an excuse for Haman's crimes.

Point being, Haman was more than a pawn and more than an isolated plot point. As much as anything else, he demonstrated something deeply true about the way the world works. Not merely that power corrupts, but that the love of power has a corrosive quality that destroys. As Wallace says, that's true of anything. Love of beauty will leave you crippled with fear at the loss of your beauty. Love of money will leave you always feeling as though you're in poverty. "Pretty much anything else you worship will eat you alive."

FINDING STRENGTH IN WEAKNESS

Esther's story reveals something else: embracing weakness has a way of inoculating yourself against a love of power, or for that matter, a corrosive love of anything else. In the biblical text, it's a little difficult to notice, because the story seems to just keep going. It seems as if Esther was pleading for her people on the same night she exposed Haman to the king, but she wasn't. Esther 8:3 says, "Then Esther spoke again to the king. She fell at his feet and wept and pleaded with him to avert the evil plan of Haman the Agagite." Once he was convinced to do so, the king's scribes were summoned, and Mordecai wrote the second edict. Here, we're given the date of these events—the twenty-third day of the month of Sivan, the third month of the year. The edict to kill the Jews was written in the month of Nisan, the first month of the year. Mordecai made his appeal to Esther at that time, and she agreed to risk her life three days after that. So, two months passed between Esther's first appeal (and Haman's execution) and Esther's second appeal.

These aren't small details, though they're easily missed. It means that Esther risked her life not once, but twice on behalf of God's people.

It demonstrates a deep principle: Once you've embraced your mortality, once you've stared death in the face, it becomes very easy to do so again. Once Esther found her place among God's people and cried, "If I perish, I perish," she was able to do it again two months later when King Ahasuerus (King Headache) seemed to have missed the point. She had once and for all embraced her own death, and now she clung to nothing—not her place in the palace, not even her life.

Here lie the keys to resisting idolatry in all its forms: a love for others, and an embrace of mortality.

When we commit ourselves to a life of deep love and compassion, we'll discover a light that far outshines the allure of idols. One can hardly imagine Mother Teresa being captivated by beauty, power, or money—though these things surely tempted and haunted her, as they do all of us. But more than anything, she was captured by a way of seeing the world that meant seeing Jesus in the faces of the poor and the sick, and that vision was powerful enough to steer the course of her life. Much of that life was spent in deep depression and darkness, but even through those shadows, love of others compelled her.

I once heard philosopher Cornel West say, "To love is to die." It most certainly means to embrace death. It means to throw yourself in harm's way out of compassion for the world around you, and out of the conviction that giving your life away is better than clinging to it. We see that in Mordecai's warning to Esther:

should she fail to identify with God's people, she and her father's house would perish.

Life consists of a choice between death and death. There is the death of the body—through sickness, self-sacrifice, or old age—and there is the death of the soul, which comes when we cling to life for our own sake. Our lives are meant to be *spent* in this world, poured out like Jesus' own. We're meant for meaningful risk, not for mere self-protection.

And therein lies our way forward in a world gone mad. Nothing could be more countercultural than this: embracing mortality, turning our lives outward, putting ourselves in harm's way.

The alternatives are all ways of seeking power. We can withdraw and attempt to consolidate power within a close, religious enclave. We can cry victimhood and attempt to elicit enough sympathy to turn things in our favor. We can cry war and embrace a political battle head-on. Or we can identify with God's people, seek the good of the city, and meaningfully risk our lives in the process. Being outsiders, we might face shame, ridicule, or worse. But we do it anyway. That's the definition of risk.

MORDECAI'S FINAL ACT

There's one final counterintuitive twist to the story of Esther, and it's in the book's final verses:

And all the acts of his power and might, and the full account of the high honor of Mordecai, to which the king advanced him, are they not written in the Book of the Chronicles of the kings of Media and Persia? For Mordecai the Jew was second in rank to King Ahasuerus, and he was great among the Jews and popular with the multitude of his brothers, for he sought the welfare of his people and spoke peace to all his people. (Est. 10:2–3)

While these books of chronicles don't remain, there are actually several references to Mordecai in the archeological remains of ancient Persia. Not only was he said to have served Xerxes, he was located in Susa, the wintertime palace and part-time residence of the king. It's significant that the name of a vizier like this survives. It offers the story some historical weight. But the greatness of Mordecai and his preservation in the archeological record is not the surprise.

What might we imagine today, should similar circumstances unfold? A politician or a businessperson has a religious awakening and leads a culture-shaping revival? What might come next? Is it at all surprising that Mordecai returned to politics and didn't become a prophet? Or at least some kind of leader among the Jews?

I don't think we should take this for granted. Mordecai returned to the palace and took up a place of leadership in the midst of a kingdom where likely many hated him for being a Jew. He worked hard, worked brilliantly, and earned tremendous honor amid the kingdom.

It strikes me as counterintuitive that a religious hero like this didn't, to borrow a more modern phrase, "go into the ministry" after his awakening. Instead, he went back into a broader cultural space, and by so doing made the realm a more peaceful place. It's the ultimate expression of Jeremiah 29—working for the good of the city, and it's an important reminder that God doesn't call everyone who takes him seriously into ministry. Perhaps one of the best things we can do to serve Christians in a culture like ours is to work for influence, to try to bring a greater sense of "peace in the realm" to our cities and communities.

THE END OF ESTHER AND THE END OF TIME

There is a reasonable claim to be made that the end of Esther refutes everything else that I've said so far about the meaning of the book of Esther and its application to our lives. After all this talk of humility, vulnerability, and self-sacrifice, the book ends with the Jews taking up arms and slaughtering their enemies. It is violence, in the end, that protects them from the wrath of the empire.

Have I missed the point?

I don't think so. Because here, we need once again to read the book in the light of the whole story of the Bible. Fundamental to God's covenant with Abraham was the promise that his descendants would be as innumerable as the stars. The preservation of the Jews throughout the Old Testament was often a bloody affair, and the end of Esther is no exception. It is just this preservation that led to the birth of Jesus, and it was the death and resurrection of Jesus that enabled Gentiles to be "grafted in" to the line of Abraham (Rom. 11). If you are a member of the church, you are a beneficiary of the wars waged to preserve Israel.

It's true that there is a shift in the way of God's people after the incarnation. Jesus taught us to love enemies, bless those who persecute us, and turn the other cheek (Matt. 5:39–44). But he didn't repudiate the laws that had come before; he fulfilled them. He summarized the law with the command to love God and love your neighbor (Luke 10:25–28), a summary embodied by Esther herself, whose love of God and neighbor enabled her act of self-sacrifice.

So, there are the events themselves and the conditions that made them possible. There is the two-day war between the Jews and their enemies, and there is the Christlike sacrifice of Esther that made victory for the Jews possible. The war itself paved a way for a greater, more complete peace that comes from Jesus.

Still not convinced? Let me add another layer.

The aftermath of the two-day war transformed Persia. Esther 9:16 says the Jews "got relief from their enemies." The realm was a far safer place to be a Jew than it was days before.

Point being, the end of Esther, like Esther's own story, is more than historical. It's a signpost. There's a time coming when we, too, will get relief from our enemies. Only, our real enemies are not political. Let's get specific: They are not hostile atheists or militant secularists, contemporary Pharisees or religious revisionists who want to rewrite the church's doctrine. Our enemies are not flesh and blood at all. They are rulers, authorities, cosmic powers, and spiritual forces of evil (Eph. 6:12). The peace in the realm that came after the Jews defeated their enemies was a foreshadowing of the time when the peace of the kingdom of God will settle in the new heaven and the new earth, a time when war, death, disease, and darkness itself will be driven out of the world.

But there is yet one more layer to consider. Esther's initial appeal to the king resulted in life after death for her alone. Her death sentence was lifted when the king ordered the death of Haman. But life after death for the Jews came after Esther's second appeal to the king (her "second coming," so to speak) and after a fierce battle that was fought throughout Persia.

This battle is eschatological—a foreshadowing of the final things that the Scriptures promise. Just as Esther pointed to the self-sacrificing intercession of Jesus, the battle between the anti-Semitic Persians and the Jews points to the battle that will ultimately shape the fate of the cosmos. The time mentioned earlier, when darkness is driven from the earth, comes at the *end* of the book of Revelation, after twenty chapters of struggle and war between the forces of good and evil.

And when the thousand years are ended, Satan will be released from his prison and will come out to deceive the nations that are at the four corners of the earth, Gog and Magog, to gather them for battle; their number is like the sand of the sea. And

they marched up over the broad plain of the earth and surrounded the camp of the saints and the beloved city, but fire
came down from heaven and consumed them, and the devil
who had deceived them was thrown into the lake of fire and
sulfur where the beast and the false prophet were, and they will
be tormented day and night forever and ever. (Rev. 20:7–10)

It's easy to skip to chapter 21 of Revelation, when all the tears
are dried and mourning and crying and pain are no more. But
such peace comes at a cost, and that cost is paid by the blood of
Jesus, who leads the saints into battle riding on a white horse and
wearing a robe dipped in blood. We cannot escape—nor should
we attempt to escape—the violent imagery of the Scriptures. But
we also shouldn't mistake the battle lines. Where Israel fought
its neighbors to preserve God's promise, we fight *on behalf* of
our neighbors to preserve God's promise. We push against the
darkness of the world in a struggle of the spirit, and neither the
powers of darkness nor the gates of hell can resist the advancing
of God's kingdom.

This, too, reframes the way we see ourselves in the world.
Our belligerent neighbors, the hostile factions and anti-Christian
political crusaders, the powers that be in the world of media, education, and the arts, the evangelists for secularism and sexual
liberation: These are not our enemies. They are, in fact, prisoners
of a much larger, darker kingdom, and we can fight for their freedom by declaring war not against them, but war on their behalf.

How? We pray. We bear witness to another world. We seek

the good of their/our cities. We put ourselves in harm's way. We look for opportunities to lay down our lives on behalf of those enemies, and we do it. We recognize that in Christ, we're already dead, so there's nothing left to lose.

CHAPTER 9

REMEMBERING

ACT NINE: ESTHER 9:20-10:3

When the battles ended, the Jews celebrated. In the outer provinces, they rested and feasted on the fourteenth day of the month of Adar. In Susa, the fighting continued through that day, so they rested and feasted on the fifteenth day.

In the months that followed, Mordecai and Esther sent letters to the Jews throughout Persia, declaring the fourteenth and fifteenth days of Adar a religious festival. From now on, from generation to generation, Jews would remember these days, remember that Haman had cast lots (*pur*) for their lives, and God had rescued them. The festival would be called Purim, and it would be the first new religious festival inaugurated for the Jews since the days of Moses. Purim is celebrated with vigor to this day.

PURIM AND RENEWAL

Yoram Hazony describes how the Persian exile was a unique time for Jews. The opportunity for assimilation—for the first time since the inauguration of their code of laws was enacted at Sinai—provided them with a choice. They didn't *have* to be Jews anymore. Hazony wrote:

> It was only after the dispersal throughout Babylonia and Persia that an individual born as a Jew found himself in immediate, constant, and personal contact with other possible identities— and had to choose for himself whether Jewishness would be something he would maintain, or something he would hide.[1]

According to Hazony, in Persia, after all the events of the book of Esther, the Jewish people experienced a "refounding . . . on an entirely different basis."[2] They now could *choose* whether or not to remain Jews, and after the miracle of their salvation, the religion was renewed. For this reason, the celebration of Purim became deeply important to the Jewish people. It is, writ large, a celebration of the kind of awakening that Mordecai and Esther experienced more intimately. It is a remembrance of when the Jews in exile were not only redeemed from a death sentence, but renewed in their commitment to their identity as God's people. This moment, like so many in the Old Testament, was a time of revival and renewal. But, as Hazony points out, it is also unique. Mordecai and Esther were not the only assimilated Jews in the empire. The cultural gravity pulled every Jew toward assimilation. The crisis, the war, and the celebration that followed were a kind of crossroads. Should they choose to see the events as the intervention of Yahweh, preserving them once again, or should they wipe their brows, be glad they'd dodged a bullet, and get on with their lives?

Purim was inaugurated as a way of saying, "Never forget." The holiday reminds Jews of the mercy of God in protecting them from the murderous ambitions of their enemies, and of their unique identity as God's people. Mordecai and Esther saw the need to guard future generations from the kind of assimilation they themselves had succumbed to. And by making the remembrance law, they created an annual, rhythmic call to remembering and celebrating God's preserving grace.

THE PRACTICES OF PURIM

At Purim, the book of Esther is read, a celebratory feast is held, and people give gifts to the poor. And, as noted earlier, in most traditions the celebration begins by reading this passage from Deuteronomy:

> "Remember what Amalek did to you on the way as you came out of Egypt, how he attacked you on the way when you were faint and weary, and cut off your tail, those who were lagging behind you, and he did not fear God. Therefore when the LORD your God has given you rest from all your enemies around you, in the land that the LORD your God is giving you for an inheritance to possess, you shall blot out the memory of Amalek from under heaven; you shall not forget." (Deut. 25:17–19)

This passage serves as a reminder that the conflict at the heart of Esther stretches back through history. Then the book of Esther itself is read aloud. Each time Haman's name is heard, the crowd boos, hisses, shouts, and rings noisemakers. Listeners are attempting literally to "blot out the name of Haman." Thus, Purim celebrations are often rowdy, including carnival-like parties, performances, masquerade parties, and even beauty contests.

In a controversial passage of the Talmud, Jews are instructed to drink wine until they can't tell the difference between the phrases "Cursed is Haman" and "Blessed is Mordecai,"[3] which means that many Purim celebrations involve a lot of throwing up. (I do not commend this particular tradition.)

Another tradition is the baking of three-cornered hamantaschen—three-cornered pastries that are filled with jelly. They represent (according to various traditions) Haman's three-cornered hat, or his pockets (the pastries' filling represents the treasure promised to the king), or—in a grimmer version— Haman's ears. According to this last version of the tradition, the ears of a condemned man would be severed before his execution. Grim, I know.

Another variation on the "meaning" of the pastries is more broadly about the book of Esther itself. The filling is "hidden," just as Esther's identity was hidden, and as God himself is hidden throughout the book. Eating the pastries is a way to celebrate the layers of revelation and awakening that take place in the story.

Twenty-five hundred years after the events of this book, people still gather yearly to remember how God preserved Israel through this crisis. It is remarkable.

CHRISTIANS AND PURIM

There are several things Christians can learn from Purim. First, it's a celebration that's part of our inheritance of faith. God's faithfulness to the Jews leads directly to his faithfulness to us in Jesus, and we should treasure it for that reason alone. Moreover, it reminds us that there has always been opposition to God's people, and it reminds us of the triumph of the faithful in a faithless world.

It can be a despair-inducing thing to watch the culture

around us decay into a more deeply secular and hostile place. It is a world where doubt is kind of a default setting, even for Christians, and we must constantly push against it—and that's without taking into account the resistance we might experience outside of ourselves. Purim is a celebration that reminds us that no matter how dark things get, there is reason to hope.

On an even more personal level, Purim is a call to reawakening. Esther and Mordecai were compromised, assimilated Persians who awoke to their Jewish identity and took bold steps on behalf of God's people. Their story rivals the apostle Paul's as a story of surprising redemption. It is a cliché, but it is true: there is no one who has gone too far to be written out of God's story.

Finally, Purim reveals the importance of formative traditions. It is, in a sense, the celebration that is meant to re-inaugurate all of the other traditions in Judaism. It exists because Mordecai and Esther understood that being counted among God's people was ultimately about more than the in-the-moment decisions they'd made.

On this point, we once again have to take issue with the Sunday school version of the story. Or rather, in this case, we might call it the Sunday Night Revival version of the story.

When I told a friend I was writing about the book of Esther, he groaned and said, "Please don't call it 'For Such a Time as This.'" This is, of course, the oft-quoted phrase that Mordecai spoke to Esther when persuading her to approach the king. It was his way of saying, "Maybe all of the events of our lives have led us to this moment." And he was correct: providence had led them to that particular crossroads, and God saved his people because of it. But the phrase is problematic for two reasons. First, it has become overused and saccharine, fodder for the worst kind of overemotional pleading in contemporary Christian music and revivalist altar calls. Second, it can give us the wrong impression about how faith works.

If we ignore Purim, then Esther's story is about life's big, critical moments, and the spirituality of the book could be misperceived. It would be about making the right decision at the right time, a revivalistic call to spiritual awakening. There's nothing wrong with that, per se, but we need to keep Purim in the mix in order to have a fuller picture of where the spirituality of Esther's story is leading us. The book doesn't end with the victory in battle. It ends with the inauguration of Purim—a new tradition meant to preserve the story for the generations to come.

Purim, then, says as much about the spirituality of the book of Esther as "for such a time as this." Yes, the critical moments of our life, when we must choose whether or not to identify with God's people, matter deeply. And yes, we need spiritual awakening. But the rest of life matters too, and identifying as one of God's people isn't just about a decision; it's about a way of life. Purim invites us to see it that way. It's a rhythm built into the calendar to remind us that our identity is easily forgotten, that the enemy is prowling and hungry, and that no matter what, God preserves his people.

PURIM AND FAITHFUL
WITNESS TODAY

I can't help but think about the church today when I read about Purim. We face immense pressure to assimilate to the culture around us, and many of us are far down the road to being neo-Persians. The church itself, though, is in its own dark place. Here's what I mean.

When Christians make the case for why we can't change our beliefs about human sexuality, or about the value of the unborn, or about other contested cultural issues, we lean on the fact that the church's doctrine is part of a two-thousand-year-old inheritance. And yet, how plausible is that argument when the culture of the church is far removed from that history? I'm thinking especially of evangelicalism—my own tradition—where in the name of contextualization, we've embraced so many aspects of a celebrity-driven, consumeristic, and techno-cratic culture. Is an argument from history persuasive coming from a church that looks nothing like the church of history? Whose members know none of its creeds and lack training in core practices? Whose holidays have been co-opted by consumerism? If an existential crisis were to strike us and one of our leaders called for a fast, would we even know what to do?

Here, I confess to having far more questions than answers, but it strikes me as deeply urgent in the years to come that the church reckon with this gap. We need to find our way back to elements of our tradition that help us as Christians to grow deep roots, connecting with those who've gone before us, and stabilizing us in the midst of a world gone mad.

These resources exist. Just as Purim is a storytelling holiday, the life of the church is marked by storytelling, from Advent to Christmas, Lent to Easter. The church's liturgy, historically, was meant to reenact the gospel through Scripture reading, prayer, preaching, and the Lord's Supper. I could go on and on, but the simple point is this: the resources are there, a deep and wonderful heritage that can shape our lives around the story of God's salvation through Jesus.

Every bit as much as we need an awakening to call us out of our assimilated stupor, we need revived traditions to form in us a way of life that is distinct, bold, and bears witness to a better world than the madhouse around us.

I know that I need both.

I know that, as much as I'd like to think otherwise, I'm assimilated into this secular age as much as the next guy. Awareness of a problem doesn't keep you from it any more than knowing it's flu season doesn't keep you from getting the flu.

I often wonder what it might feel like to come totally alive to God in this life. I think of Paul's advice to "pray unceasingly" (1 Thess. 5:17 DARBY), or the missionary Frank Laubach's "game with minutes,"[4] in which he trained himself to turn his thoughts to God every minute of every day. I think of the powerful spiritual presence of older saints who've devoted their lives to seeking God's face: the wisdom they share, the peace they exude, the vulnerability they experience both in their aging bodies and their battered souls. I long for that peace and that life-giving presence.

It's hard not to see the corollary between their suffering and their grace. There's no doubt that some of that journey comes through suffering. That was certainly true of Mordecai and Esther. One cannot imagine them as the founders of a twenty-five-hundred-year-old religious festival apart from their encounter with death. There is a bridge between our suffering and our awakening.

It's also hard not to see the need for time. The most beautiful souls I know have spent decades in prayer. Life, though it's too often cut short, is typically a long project, and life with God becomes its richest over a long, slow journey. Here is why we need Purim—or rather, why we need a lifelong plan of remembering our story of redemption.

THE WAY BACK HOME

This is Esther's road map for life with God. It is, in a sense, a map drawn to help us find our way back home. I believe that's why God is "hidden" throughout the story. It is the story of a group of people finding their way back to God through a darkened world; finding their voice for faithful, vulnerable witness; and seeking to ensure that the generations after them don't make the same mistake.

Maybe you read this and feel as though you don't need the

lessons Esther offers. You don't need the awakening. You don't need to take the time to honestly assess how assimilated you might be. I can say with all sincerity: good for you.

But I need it. And I need the help finding my way home again. And I'll probably need that help for the rest of my life. I also need help finding the courage to stand while the world around me bows to idols, the courage to die rather than live an empty life of numbness.

Most of all, I need the hope it offers for faith among the faithless. Sometimes, that phrase is good for describing the gap between Christians and the world around them. But sometimes— and perhaps more often—it describes God himself at work in a world gone mad. Because the darkness overwhelms me, and my own faith fades all too often. But "if we are faithless, he remains faithful" (2 Tim. 2:13).

I may not see his hand or hear his name, but I know he hasn't left us.

ACKNOWLEDGMENTS

No one just locks himself in an empty room and writes a book. Even if he did, he'd carry the voices and visions of life outside those walls. Otherwise, it simply wouldn't be a book worth reading.

For this book, some specific acknowledgments are necessary. The first is Tim Keller, for his 2007 sermon "If I Perish, I Perish." The second is the Jewish philosopher Yoram Hazony, for his book *God and Politics in Esther* (cited herein). Together, these two men opened up the story of Esther in more ways than I can count, and most of this book bears their influence. Keller's Christological reading of the book shaped much of my overarching idea about weakness and vulnerability. Hazony's understanding of compromise and assimilation, as well as his rich understanding of Esther's place within the Jewish canon, shaped the way I see these characters profoundly. Lastly,

Hazony's footnotes led me into the Talmud, where I found perspectives on Esther I wouldn't have known otherwise.

Additional thanks go to Gregory Thornbury, who allowed me to preach on Esther years ago at Union University, and who encouraged me to keep thinking and working on this text.

Thanks to Kevin Jamison for reading some early drafts.

Thanks to Don Gates for helping guide this project along.

Thanks to Webster Younce and the fine folks at Thomas Nelson.

Thanks most of all to Sarah, Maggie, and Dorothy. I hope this story gives you the strength to be weak, and the confidence in God's faithfulness in the midst of this crazy world.

ABOUT THE AUTHOR

Mike Cosper is the executive director of Harbor Media, a nonprofit media company serving Christians in a post-Christian world. He served for sixteen years as a pastor at Sojourn Community Church in Louisville, Kentucky, and is the author of *Recapturing the Wonder*, *The Stories We Tell*, and *Rhythms of Grace*. He lives with his family in Louisville, Kentucky.

NOTES

INTRODUCTION
1. Robert Robinson, "Come, Thou Fount of Every Blessing," 1757, v. 4.
2. Martin Luther, *Table Talk*, trans. William Hazlitt (Grand Rapids: Christian Classics Ethereal Library, 2004), sec. 24.
3. Walker Percy, *The Message in the Bottle: How Queer Man Is, How Queer Language Is, and What One Has to Do with the Other* (n.p.: Open Road Media, 2011), chap. 1.

CHAPTER 1: EMPIRE OF IDOLS
1. See, for example, Ian MacGregor Morris, *Xerxes: King of Kings: The True Story* (n.p.: Pen and Sword, forthcoming).
2. Yehuda T. Radday, in Karen H. Jobes, *The NIV Application Commentary: Esther* (Grand Rapids: Zondervan, 1999), 58.
3. Richard Stoneman, *Xerxes: A Persian Life* (New Haven, CT: Yale University Press, 2015), 153.
4. *The William Davidson Talmud* on Sefaria, Megillah 11b:12 (public domain), https://www.sefaria.org/Megillah.11b.12?lang=bi.
5. See her book of the same name. Pamela Paul, *Pornified: How*

Pornography Is Damaging Our Lives, Our Relationships, and Our Families (New York: Times Books, 2005).

6. See James K. A. Smith's fantastic book *You Are What You Love: The Spiritual Power of Habit* (Grand Rapids: Brazos, 2016), especially chapter 2, "You Might Not Love What You Think."

7. James K. A. Smith, *You Are What You Love*, 11–12.

CHAPTER 2: CONQUEST AND COMPROMISE

1. Yoram Hazony, *God and Politics in Esther* (New York: Cambridge University Press, 2016), 18.

2. "Jackie Mason on Being Jewish," YouTube video, 3:38, posted by Justin White, December 1, 2014, https://www.youtube.com /watch?v=jeVTtfk0oI8.

3. Eugene Peterson, *As Kingfishers Catch Fire: A Conversation on the Ways of God Formed by the Words of God* (Colorado Springs: Waterbrook, 2017), 36.

4. A great exploration of this phenomenon, including its religious implications, is Bill Bishop's *The Big Sort: Why the Clustering of Like-Minded America Is Tearing Us Apart* (New York: Mariner, 2009).

5. James K. A. Smith, "How My Millennial Students Found Their 'Hitchhiker's Guide' to a Secular Age," *World Post*, updated November 27, 2016, http://www.huffingtonpost.com/entry /charles-taylor-philosopher_us_58067afde4b0180a36e700f3.

6. Anything helpful I have to say about this passage came from Tim Keller. For example, see his sermon "Serving the City," YouTube video, 31:27, the eighth sermon in Redeemer Presbyterian Church's series "Where We Are Going: The City and the Mission," posted by Gospel in Life, April 18, 2016, https://www.youtube.com/watch?v=2ziAJXT7gok.

7. Victoria Woollaston, "How Often Do YOU Check Your Phone? Average User Picks Up Their Device 85 Times a DAY—Twice as Often as They Realise," *Daily Mail*, October 29, 2015, http:

//www.dailymail.co.uk/sciencetech/article-3294994/How-check
-phone-Average-user-picks-device-85-times-DAY-twice-realise
.html.

8. See Christy Wampole's comments on the embrace of irony in
"How to Live Without Irony," *Opinionator* (blog), *New York
Times*, November 17, 2012, https://opinionator.blogs.nytimes
.com/2012/11/17/how-to-live-without-irony/.

CHAPTER 3: THE GIRL WITH TWO NAMES

1. Rabbi Meir in *The William Davidson Talmud*, Megillah 13a,
Sefaria, accessed August 30, 2017, https://www.sefaria.org
/Megillah.13a?lang=bi.

2. Esther Rabbah 6.8.

3. Lance Williams, "Sexual Abuse Prevalence in the United States,"
Mending the Soul, accessed August 30, 2017, http://mendingthesoul
.org/research-and-resources/research-and-articles/sexual-abuse
-prevalence-in-the-united-states/?gclid=CInZq-vI7dMCFQEE
aQod-HUNKQ.

4. Susan Dominus, "Is an Open Marriage a Happier Marriage?"
New York Times Magazine, May 11, 2017, https://www.nytimes
.com/2017/05/11/magazine/is-an-open-marriage-a-happier
-marriage.html?hp&action=click&pgtype=Homepage&click
Source=story-heading&module=photo-spot-region&region=top
-news&WT.nav=top-news&_r=0.

CHAPTER 4: RESISTANCE

1. Donald Langmead and Christine Garnaut, *Encyclopedia of
Architectural and Engineering Feats* (2001), s.v. "Persepolis," 45.

2. Hazony, *God and Politics in Esther*, 68 (see chap. 2, n. XX).

3. Hazony, *God and Politics in Esther*, 32–34.

4. See her ten "guideposts" for wholehearted living in Brené Brown,
*Daring Greatly: How the Courage to Be Vulnerable Transforms the
Way We Live, Love, Parent, and Lead* (n.p.: Avery, 2012), 9–10.

5. David Brooks wrote helpfully on this topic in an article titled "The Strange Persistence of Guilt," *New York Times*, March 31, 2017, https://www.nytimes.com/2017/03/31/opinion/the-strange -persistence-of-guilt.html?_r=0.

6. René Girard, *I See Satan Fall Like Lightning* (Maryknoll, NY: Orbis, 2001), 164.

7. Derek Rishmawy, "How Do We Stop Weaponizing Our Victims?" *Reformedish* (blog), September 8, 2015, https://derekzrishmawy .com/2015/09/08/how-do-we-stop-weaponizing-our-victims/.

8. Andy Crouch, *Strong and Weak: Embracing a Life of Love, Risk and True Flourishing* (Downers Grove, IL: IVP, 2016), 41.

CHAPTER 5: THE PLOT

1. Hazony, *God and Politics in Esther*, 73.

2. Slavoj Žižek, *Violence: Six Sideways Reflections* (New York: Picador, 2008), 46–47.

3. See Joe Carter's introductory article on Sanger, "9 Things You Should Know About Planned Parenthood Founder Margaret Sanger" Gospel Coalition, October 18, 2016, https://www .thegospelcoalition.org/article/9-things-you-should-know-about -planned-parenthood-founder-margaret-sanger.

4. See her book, *Eichmann in Jerusalem* (New York: Viking, 1963), and her subsequent reflections in the foreword of her later work *The Life of the Mind* (n.p.: Harcourt, 1978). Her view is not without controversy or dispute, but I find her argument very compelling.

5. Arendt, *The Life of the Mind*, 4.

6. See Karen Swallow Prior, "Loving Our Pro-Choice Neighbors in Word and Deed," *Christianity Today*, December 2015, http://www .christianitytoday.com/women/2015/december/loving-our-pro -choice-neighbors-in-word-and-deed.html.

7. Karen Swallow Prior, "Loving Our Pro-Choice Neighbors in Word and Deed."

8. See Hannah Arendt, "The Victory of the *Animal Laborans*," chap. 45 in *The Human Condition*, 2nd ed. (Chicago: University of Chicago, 1998), chap. 45, 320–25.

9. Andy Crouch, *Culture Making: Recovering Our Creative Calling* (Downers Grove, IL: IVP, 2008), 200.

CHAPTER 6: THE CROSSROADS

1. Jobes, *The* NIV *Application Commentary*, 131–32 (see chap. 1, n. XX).

2. Dante Alighieri, *The Divine Comedy*, trans. Clive James (City: Publisher, Year), Page/Number Range.

3. These lectures were gathered together in an audiobook. See Brené Brown, *The Power of Vulnerability: Teachings on Authenticity, Connection, and Courage* (n.p.: Sounds True, 2013).

CHAPTER 7: THE THRONE ROOM

1. See Karen Jobes's discussion of this in Esther in *The* NIV *Application Commentary* (Grand Rapids: Zondervan, 1999), Kindle edition, loc. 2527.

2. For the full story of the prodigal son, see Luke 15:11–32.

3. See Tim Keller's sermon from April 22, 2007, "If I Perish, I Perish," available from the resource site Gospel in Life, at http://www.gospelinlife.com/if-i-perish-i-perish-5538.

CHAPTER 8: THE FEASTS, THE HONOR, AND THE DOWNFALL

1. David Foster Wallace, "This Is Water" (commencement address, Kenyon College, Gambier, Ohio, May 21, 2005), accessed July 29, 2017, https://web.ics.purdue.edu/~drkelly/DFWKenyonAddress2005.pdf.

CHAPTER 9: REMEMBERING

1. Hazony, *God and Politics in Esther*, 165 (see chap. 2, n. XX).

2. Hazony, *God and Politics in Esther*, 165 (see chap. 2, n. XX).

3. Babylonian Talmud, Megillah 7b.

4. See Frank Laubach's *Letters from a Modern Mystic* (New York: Student Volunteer Movement, 1937), online at http://www .howtolovegod.org/wp-content/uploads/2012/02/Letters-By-A -Modern-Mystic.pdf.